A Handbook On
Becoming A
TRUE
Professional

How to develop the Discipline & Attributes
that will make you a TRUE PROFESSIONAL

Copyright © 2007, 2010
by Candido Segarra

WWW.FORESIGHTPUBLISHINGNOW.COM

*A Handbook on Becoming a True Professional—
How to Develop the Disciplines and Attributes That Will Make You
a True Professional by Candido Segarra*

Printed in the United States of America

ISBN 0-9844423-1-6

All rights reserved solely by the author. The author guarantees all contents are original and do not infringe upon the legal rights of any other person or work. No part of this book may be reproduced in any form without the permission of the author. The views expressed in this book are not necessarily those of the publisher.

TABLE OF CONTENTS

Introduction X
Chapter 1 Be on Time All the Time 15
Chapter 2 Become a Good Communicator 19
Chapter 3 Be Reliable 25
Chapter 4 Learning Never Ends for the Professional 29
Chapter 5 Dress for Credibility 33
Chapter 6 Attitude 41
Chapter 7 Respect for the Hierarchy of Authority 47
Chapter 8 Proper Business Etiquette 51
Chapter 9 Strong Knowledge of Your Company & Products 57
Chapter 10 Personal Organization Skills 61
Chapter 11 Sharpening Your Time Management Skills 65
Chapter 12 Discipline 73
Chapter 13 Self-Control 79
Chapter 14 Good Communication and Presentation Skills 83
Chapter 15 Temperance 91
Chapter 16 Unselfishness 95
Chapter 17 Ability and Disposition to Train Others and to Delegate 99
Chapter 18 Customer Satisfaction Attitude 103
Chapter 19 Leadership by Example 107
Chapter 20 Keep an Attitude of Excellence 113
Chapter 21 Health 117
Chapter 22 Teamwork 123
Chapter 23 Effective Project Management 127
Chapter 24 Taking Personal Responsibility..................................133
Chapter 25 Avoiding Rude Behavior 137
Chapter 26 Conflict Resolution 141
Chapter 27 Boundaries 145
Chapter 28 Getting Hired 153
Chapter 29 Let's Start With Our Identity 159
Chapter 30 Integrity: Acting What You Believe 165
Chapter 31 Life Values and Legacy 173

ACKNOWLEDGMENTS

Writing a book is a great challenge. I have been blessed with many people in my life that helped me through the journey. I would like to give special thanks to Jim Robinson, for your trust, unconditional commitment, support and encouragement; I treasure our friendship.

A special recognition to Barbara Ruiz for your vision, enthusiasm, belief and energy in making Foresight Publishing Group, Inc. a success. Thank you Tom Shwaegerle for your tireless efforts, you're on-target insights, professionalism and vision; you have been key in developing our world class management development training program.

To my editors Tom Taylor, Brian Mast and most especially, to my Editor in Chief, my wife, Cathy for the many hours of dedication and love in making this book as error-free as possible.

For my dear friend and Pastor Dr. Norm Wise for always being there when we needed you.

To our children Michelle, Juan, Jorge, Viviana and Katelyn for inspiring me day by day to be a better man. In their young careers I see in them the attributes of a true professional.

To all of my clients, too many to mention by name. My heart is full of gratitude and humility for your trust and support you have given me through the years. I have learned so many valuable lessons through our association!

To my God:

He is my refuge and my fortress in whom I trust-Psalm 91

To Cathy:

my wife and best friend and closest companion you are a nurturer of my God given dreams. You are sensitive, loving and genuine. I love what I am when I am with you. Thank you for being effective at the family tasks that sustain our common life. I love my experience with you.

Introduction

Pro•fes•sion: a calling requiring specialized knowledge and often long and intensive academic preparation; b: a principal calling, vocation, or employment; c: the whole body of persons engaged in a calling.

Pro•fes•sion•al: engaged in one of the learned professions c (1): characterized by or conforming to the technical or ethical standards of a profession (2): exhibiting a courteous, conscientious, and generally businesslike manner in the workplace.

During my thirty-six year professional career in business, I have had the opportunity to know and work with many highly professional people, as well as with many not-so-professional individuals.

As I talk about professionalism, I'm not referring to specialized knowledge or long and intensive training. This book is about the attributes, qualities, characteristics, and character traits that define a person in any given profession. In other words, I'm talking about the second definition, not the first.

Professionalism as a work ethic and a character trait is fast becoming a rare commodity at every position level and in every organization. We don't learn how to become a true professional through a college curriculum and we rarely see it modeled within many organizations today.

I was inspired to write this book for three main reasons:
1. To help emerging generations of new professionals to recognize and choose to embrace and practice the standards of professional conduct which will become their lifetime standards;
2. To encourage experienced professionals to practice and develop skills which will lead them to new levels of professionalism, by identifying the attributes that constitute true professionalism;

3. Out of my personal frustration with my own shortcomings and by observing and feeling frustrated by the low standards and lack of professionalism in the workplace. I have also been inspired and encouraged by the strengths and desire to become a true professional, which I have noticed among many of the hundreds of professionals I have trained in management and leadership skills over the years.

I strongly believe that everyone, regardless of the career or field of choice, envisions becoming the best that they could be as a professional. Many people long to be admired and respected by others, as they identify themselves through their professions with those traits, that in their own view, make a person "successful".

But few really understand what it really means to be a truly successful professional, much less how to become one. Professionalism is something that we become; it is a process determined by who we are. Being a true professional is a personal character trait, not a description of our profession or how well we perform the technical aspects of our trade, or how we look or act like.

No matter how many years of vocational experience we may have, becoming a true professional is a personal choice, a discipline, as well as a personal responsibility.

In order to better understand professionalism, it is important to be able to identify what the attributes and characteristics are that define the character traits and good habits of a true professional, as well as what sets them apart from most other people.

This book is not intended to be an encyclopedia of all the topics covered, but rather a useful reference handbook, an eye opener, of the areas you should pay attention to and practice, in order to become a true professional.

You will also find at the end of the book, the attributes, characteristics and experiences that many CEOs of successful companies have shared with me over the years, based on what they feel every admired professional should embrace.

Finally, the attributes outlined in this book are not listed in ranking order of importance. All of the attributes are important and a true professional must strive, through discipline, to develop them all. The apparent repetition in some chapters are intentional, and designed for learning retention and to stress the importance of some specific points.

It is my hope that this book will influence and stimulate your thoughts and your resolve to become a better person and a better professional.

CANDIDO SEGARRA

"Watch your thoughts; they become your words. Watch your words; they become your actions. Watch your actions; they become your habits. Watch your habits; they become your character. Watch your character for it will become your destiny."

— Frank Outlaw

Chapter 1

Be on Time All the Time

The Non-Verbal Communication of Punctuality

When we practice punctuality, we are sending various unequivocal messages. First, you are communicating that you respect other people's time. Second, you are communicating that you are trustworthy. Third, you are sending a clear message that you are consistent. Fourth, it tells that you take your job seriously and that you respect yourself. Fifth, it says that you have respect for your own time and that your time is valuable too.

A true professional is always on time for appointments. Get there at least 10 minutes before, in order to relax, catch your breath, and gather your thoughts before each appointment.

Being on time for work communicates the same message of respect, trustworthiness and consistency, which are necessary attributes, if you are expecting to advance and to be respected in the workplace.

Plan and Schedule to Be on Time All the Time

You are expected to always be punctual; otherwise, it will adversely impact your credibility; and this is true, whether the person you have the appointment with has the habit of arriving after the prearranged time or not.

When you schedule your appointments, block 60 minutes for a 30 minute meeting or 90 minute for an hour meeting, to allow for extended meetings. Leave a 30-minute time slot over the estimated driving time in between appointments. Allowing ample time between appointments will eliminate the impolite and embarrassing position of having to cancel a previously scheduled (next) appointment because your meetings have run over the time you've allocated.

If you are running late, make sure that you call your appointment to let him/her know that you are going to be late and how many minutes you are running behind. If you expect to be later than 20 minutes or more, make sure that you give the person the option of asking if he/she wants to reschedule the appointment. This shows respect and value for their time.

Show up to your meeting fully prepared and more importantly, focused and in a mental state of readiness and alertness.

Timely Preparation Before a Meeting

A true professional finishes the tasks necessary to complete their work on time, regardless of how long it takes to accomplish it and gives himself sufficient time to deal with unexpected problems. Never begin preparing for a meeting or start a project at the last minute. I'm certain that this bad habit did not work well during your college years and certainly will not serve you at all as a professional in the workplace. Always allow ample time the day before to proofread, review, correct, and prepare for all your meetings and presentations.

It's Five O'clock!

A professional is not looking at the clock for the quitting time, but makes sure that he completes as many tasks as possible scheduled for that day, before leaving his desk. Work your day, not based on the clock, but based on meeting your daily goals and tasks for the day. The key is to work your day setting realistic task-goals for each day, in order to pace yourself to the early completion of each project.

A reliable person is someone who is consistently trustworthy and who is always on time and dependable to his company and coworkers. Dependability, trustworthiness, and consistency are the result of the choices that you make on a daily basis.

"The most important thing in communication is to hear what isn't being said."

— Peter F. Drucker
American educator and writer, b.1909, d. Nov. 2005

Chapter 2

Become a Good Communicator

Whether you communicate with one person or a full audience, the ability to convey messages and mental pictures in an organized, coherent manner to influence your audience for action, is one of the most useful skills a professional can develop.

The information age has brought to the forefront the importance for professionals to be able to get your message across. Whether it is a sales presentation or report presentation, the application of simple skills, along with lots of practice, will help you become a successful presenter. The following guidelines will help you.

1. **Define the Reason:**

    Know the reason why you are making the presentation; what is it that you want to achieve? What action do you want your audience to take? What information do you want your group to know?

2. **Do Your Research:**

    Carefully and thoroughly research the subject matter of your presentation. Get your facts right. Go online and search other people's work on the subject in order to get ideas on how to present your topic, content, etc.

3. **Preparation of the Presentation:**

The use of visual materials is an essential part of every presentation, as our mind thinks in pictures, visuals and illustrations. The following are some useful tips to prepare your communications:

- Use Power Point slides, but never use more than six lines of copy per slide. Pay full attention to the contrast between your background and your fonts; a dark background with light color fonts work the best. Don't let the background be too distracting or busy. Use only two font types and two (no more than three) colors.
- Three-ring binders with clear front pocket covers (to customize the cover) are the most versatile way to present your handouts.
- If your handouts are just a few pages, try a nice presentation cover. Your local office supply warehouse carries many styles, but you can also try: www.paperdirect.com for a wide variety of more creative, fine covers and laser papers, reasonably priced.
- The more white space you have in your presentation, the better. A handout should be a quick, easy read. When typing your handouts write an outline and then, go back and expand on each point. Make your font size 16 or 18 points in Times New Roman or Arial, for easy reading.

4. **Practice:**

In order to have full control of your presentation, there is no substitute for practice,. Your success as a presenter will depend upon the amount of preparation you dedicate for yourself. The more you prepare and practice, the more confident and less nervous you are going to be. Without such preparation, there is sure to be failure. The American best selling writer, H. Jackson Brown, Jr. said: "The best preparation for tomorrow is doing your best today".

5. **The Presentation:**
- Opening: Use a powerful attention-getter opening to engage your audience and get them involved from the beginning. As an opening, use natural humor or a shocking statement, and then explain what you meant (must be related to the theme of the presentation); or ask a question and ask for a show of hands.
- Speaking Skills:
  1. Control your nerves before the presentation by closing your eyes, taking five slow deep breaths, slowly exhaling with each breath.
  2. Vary your voice pitch, tone and speed.
  3. Use gestures and body movements. Be energetic, but don't exaggerate your movements; be natural.
  4. Use stories and illustrations.
  5. Use pauses to regroup, or to make them think of a point you just made.
  6. Ask for opinions.
  7. Ask the audience for anecdotes, experiences and examples related to your presentation.
  8. Make eye contact as you present, in order to connect with your audience.
  9. Use a timer to stay on track.
  10. Involve your audience by asking questions.
- Closing:
  1. Have a powerful end. This can be a call for action, an inspirational story, or a powerful story which can help make the case of what you are presenting.
  2. Plant questions among people in the audience, in order to break the ice for other people to ask questions.
  3. When asked a question, repeat it in order to make sure you understand it.

4. After responding to a question made, make sure to ask, "Did I answer your question?" to verify the full understanding of your answer.

Influence

The art of influencing other people to action is the foundation of every presentation.

Credibility

If you don't have a "killer" resume, establish your credibility by outlining the sources of your research work. In other words, use someone else's credibility by associating and quoting them. This will let your audience know that you have done your homework in a thorough manner.

Preparation

Always over prepare. There is no substitute for solid preparation. Over preparation, solid research, and pre-meeting practice of the presentation will minimize nervousness and greatly increase confidence and presentation control.

Demeanor

Above all…be yourself:

- Use your natural gestures and hand motions in a way that your audience perceives that you are very comfortable in your own skin.
- Be energetic without going overboard.
- Use humor only if you have a natural gift for humor. Otherwise, smile and be likable in a way that is very comfortable to you.
- If you make a mistake, don't highlight it by showing nervousness or using facial histrionics. Make a short pause, admit your mistake with a short statement, quickly correct it, and move forward in the most natural way (as if it was meant to be that way).
- Vary your voice tone, pitch, and pace of the presentation to avoid monotony.

- Make eye contact with as many members of your audience as possible.
- Always stay on schedule.
- Involve your audience as much as possible through questions, short exercises, icebreakers.
- Have a very powerful ending by telling a short inspirational story or outlining the benefits or end results of what you are presenting.
- Use feedback by encouraging questions or through evaluations.

"The only lifelong, reliable motivations are those that come from within, and one of the strongest of those is the joy and pride that grow from knowing that you've just done something as well as you can do it."

— Lloyd Dobens

Chapter 3

Be Reliable

Reliability

People pay more attention to what we do than to what we say. Be a managerial leader by example, even if you are not at present a manager or a leader. Ask yourself: what are the healthy behaviors I admire, want to have and would like the people around me to copy? Then, do those things consistently until you become that.

Consistency

A consistent person is one marked by regularity of action or steady continuity of the things he says he believes, or asks other people to do, free from variation or contradiction. Consistency is a choice, a habit, an attribute, and the attitude of winners.

Apply consistency by:

- Always being prepared for meetings — there is nothing more unprofessional than watching someone come unprepared to a meeting or who tries to "wing-it" during a presentation. There is no credible substitute for preparation.
- Always being on time to a meeting or an appointment.
- Always being honest in everything you do — not sometimes, but every time.

- Always being polite and controlled.
- Always leading and managing by example.
- Always acting on your beliefs, rather than wavering to please people.

Let a Yes be a Yes; a No be a No

You can't be truthful to other people if you are not truthful to yourself. Setting boundaries is as important and healthy in business as they are in personal relationships. Don't try to please people by telling them yes, when in reality you mean that you don't know, or if you feel that you should say no. Setting limits is about telling the truth; about being truthful.

In the long run, you will never burn bridges by honestly expressing your feelings behind a "yes" or a "no" answer, as that shows character, honesty and integrity, and inner strength; attributes which most people admire. Always take responsibility by meaning what you say and letting your "yes" be a "yes" and a "no" a "no".

Become a Trustworthy Person

In the Bible (Luke 16:10-13) Jesus says that if we are honest in small things, we will be honest in big things; if we are crooked in small things, we will be a crook in big things. He poses the rhetoric question: if we are not honest in small jobs and assignments, who will put us in charge of the store?

I think He wants us to learn the lesson that responsibility and trust comes as a result of becoming responsible and trustworthy; it's a discipline to practice, which makes us, by habit, become trustworthy and reliable. It's the result of our character formation and character formation starts with a choice of what we want to practice… today.

We Learn . . .
    10% of what we read
    20% of what we hear
    30% of what we see
    50% of what we see and hear
    70% of what we discuss
    80% of what we experience
    95% of what we teach others.
— William Glasser, b.1925

CHAPTER 4

LEARNING NEVER ENDS FOR THE PROFESSIONAL

Desire to Learn

A true professional is always striving to learn more of the technical and operational aspects of their companies, and constantly shows eagerness to develop their interpersonal and managerial skills.

Experts agree that in this technological world, our knowledge base doubles every three years. Our skills today will become obsolete tomorrow. The only way to stay competitive and intelligent in this rapidly changing world is by choosing to have the attitude that the school never ends for a professional.

Learning as an Attitude

Studies show that if you have the right attitude and desire to learn, skill will follow. Learning is not an event which ends when we get a diploma. It is a lifelong process of continuous formal and informal learning, updating by reading, and learning from other people's experiences and experimentation.

Information Is Power

Or better yet, the wise application of information is power. When you become a well informed person in different areas (not only in the professional aspect) you become a source of inspiration and understanding, which other people will look and be attracted to for counsel and wisdom.

Make a habit of learning about art, history, politics, theology, anthropology, science and technology, a little at a time. Develop an inquisitive mind for life. A good place to start is an online encyclopedia. Look for short, condensed books on the different subjects in your local library. Read a chapter per day; read the whole book a piece at a time.

The idea is not for you to become an expert on each subject, but for you to learn how life works.

Enroll in as many professional seminars as you possibly can and most important, develop an action plan or specific ideas or programs you will implement when back in your workplace after each seminar.

Remember that learning is not an event (going to a seminar) but a process, which involves a specific application plan.

Intelligent conversations are based on unbiased, factual knowledge. The more educated you are on different historic, technological, cultural, political, spiritual, financial, and behavioral issues, the more intelligent your conversations will become and better yet, you will become a critical thinker.

Knowledge Is Competence, but Humility is Strength

It is beyond any discussion of fact that the more knowledge-competent you become, the more competent you will be in your profession. But remember that knowledge without humility becomes pride, which is an attribute that most people despise. The acquisition of knowledge should always be motivated and applied for the benefit of others, not to feed our own egos or to feel better about ourselves.

Learn From Other People's Experiences

Observe, listen, ask for advice, and learn from other people's experience. This attribute not only shows strength of humility, but will save you a lot of time with your own trials and errors.

Other people's trials and errors before they achieved success is an ideal way to learn what worked and didn't work for them. Read biographies of successful people in your field to profit from their experiences, their trials, perseverance and successes. These biographies can be not only an inspiration, but an excellent source of ideas.

Learn Through Experimentation and Risk Taking

The German classical scholar, philosopher Friedrich Nietzsche said, "The most instructive experiences are those of everyday life." Dare to experiment with ideas, explore new methods, techniques and dare to make mistakes. Once you learn from a mistake, it becomes a valuable tool in your toolbox of experience.

Team Learning

One of the characteristics of knowledge-building is that the sense of "we" takes the place of the sense of "I." Team learning creates synergy: a feeling that the group operating collectively is more powerful and effective than the assembly of individuals. A true leader leads the troops to learning.

He doesn't just "send" his people to a seminar; he goes with them and learns together. The language of humility says, "even if I know the material, I'm going with them to coach them and to help them understand the concept". Many training programs don't work because the leader is not there, with his team, to share the concepts and supervise its application in the workplace and coach for results... or at the very least, lead the sponsorship of the training.

Be the kind of professional that learns with the team and applies new ideas and concepts together. You will find that this is one of the smartest and most profitable ways to invest your time, even if you are a very busy individual.

You cannot climb the ladder of success dressed in the costume of failure.

— Zig Ziglar
Motivational speaker and author

CHAPTER 5

DRESS FOR CREDIBILITY

You never have a second chance for a first good impression. You should always dress the part. A true professional dresses one notch above the professional company code or peers. If they are wearing golf shirts and sport pants, you wear a sport coat, tie and dress pants. If they are wearing sport coats, wear a nice suit, etc.

The way you dress affects your attitude. The more informal you dress, the more informal your mindset will be.

The following are some very useful guidelines published by the College of Business of the University of Missouri in Columbia on their website: http://business.missouri.edu/255/default.aspx.

Business Attire Do's & Don'ts

Looking the part promises both personal and financial success. Quality garments wear longer, fit better, and therefore, save money in the long run. Above all, if your clothing projects a professional image, others will respond to you in kind.

Here are a few suggestions for maintaining the proper image:

MEN

- Do wear your suit jacket when you conduct business outside your office. Your authority travels with you.

- Do keep hair and nails clean and neat.
- Do wear appropriate jewelry.
- Do not overpower your appearance with heavy cologne!
- Do not wear short-sleeved shirts under suit coats. Showing a clean cuff is a must.
- Do not wear ankle socks or light colored socks with a dark suit.

Women

- Do wear comfortable shoes and hosiery to complement your outfit.
- Do wear natural looking makeup.
- Do wear appropriate jewelry (no bangles or dangly earrings).
- Do keep hair and nails clean and neat.
- Do not overpower your appearance with heavy perfume!
- Do not wear elaborate hairstyles.
- Do not wear jeans or casual slacks.
- Do not wear trendy fashions with built-in obsolescence.

Executive Wardrobe Tips

Men

Suits: Look for...

- Classic fabrics, patterns, and colors which are always in style and easy to accessorize.
- Contoured jacket collar that lies smoothly around the neck with no space between it and your shirt.
- Smooth, straight seams with a single row of stitching.

Suit care: Be sure to...

- Hang suits on wooden or plastic contour hangers. Leave your jacket unbuttoned and be sure to empty pockets.
- Leave space between hangers so garments will be free of wrinkles.

- Read and follow the care instructions on your garment.

Shirts: The best ones have...

- A single row of stitching along shoulder and side seams to prevent puckering.
- More stitches per inch. A quality shirt will have 15-18 stitches per inch for strength and better appearance.
- Store ties unknotted to eliminate wrinkles.

Outer coats: Keep in mind that...

- Outer coat sleeve length should cover the suit coat sleeve.
- You should sit in your outer coat in the store to be certain that it is comfortable.

Shoes:

- Wear shoes that coordinate with your suit.
- Keep shoes in good condition and polished.

WOMEN

Suits/dresses: Look for...

- Classic fabrics, patterns, and colors which are always in style and easy to accessorize.
- Dresses in solid color or conservative print.
- Contoured jacket collar that fits smoothly around the neck with no space between it and your shirt.
- Smooth, straight seams and hems.

Suit care: Be sure to...

- Hang suits on wooden or plastic contour hangers. Leave your jacket unbuttoned and be sure to empty pockets.
- Leave space between hangers so garments will be free of wrinkles.
- Read and follow the care instructions on your garment.

Blouses/shirts:

- Tailored blouses/shirts, not a lot of frills or ruffles.

- Solid color or conservative prints to coordinate with suit.

Shoes:
- Wear low-heeled pumps that coordinate with your suit/dress.
- Keep shoes clean and in good condition

What is Business Casual?
- Khaki pants, neatly pressed, and a pressed long-sleeved, buttoned solid color shirt is safe for both men and women. Polo shirts, unwrinkled, are an appropriate choice if you know the environment will be quite casual, outdoors or in a very hot location. This may not seem like terribly exciting attire, but remember you are not trying to stand out for the cutting edge look, but for your good judgment in a business environment.
- Shoes/Belt: Leather belt and leather shoes (please, no athletic shoes at receptions).
- Cost/Quality: You are not expected to be able to afford the same clothing as a CEO. However, do invest in quality that will look appropriate during your first two or three years on the job for a business casual environment or occasions.
- Details: Everything should be clean, well-pressed, and not show wear. Even the nicest khakis after 100 washings may not be your best choice for a reception. Carefully inspect new clothes for tags, and all clothes for loose threads, etc. (as with interview attire).
- Use common sense. If there is 10 inches of snow on the ground and you are rushing to an information session right after class and you left home 12 hours earlier, no one will expect you to show up looking ready for a photo shoot — they'll just be happy you made it. If you show up at an event and realize you are not as well dressed as you should be, make a quick, pleasant apology, and then make a good impression with your interpersonal skills and intelligent questions.
- A briefcase or portfolio is not usually necessary for most

business casual receptions or events.

Specifics for Men's Business Casual

- *Ties:* Ties are generally not necessary for business casual, but if you are in doubt, you can wear a tie. It never hurts to slightly overdress. By dressing nicely, you are paying your host a compliment. You can always wear the tie and discreetly walk by the room where the function is held; if no one else is wearing a tie, you can discreetly remove yours if you have a place for it such as a jacket pocket.
- *Shirts:* Long-sleeved shirts are considered dressier than short-sleeved and are appropriate even in summer. Choosing white or light blue solid or conservative stripes is your safest bet. Polo shirts, (tucked in, of course), are acceptable in more casual situations.
- *Socks:* Do wear dark socks, mid-calf length so no skin is visible when you sit down.
- *Shoes:* Leather shoes should be worn. No sandals, athletic shoes or hiking boots.
- *Facial Hair:* Just as with interviews. Facial hair, if worn, should be well groomed.
- *Jewelry:* Wear a conservative watch. If you choose to wear other jewelry, be conservative. Removing earrings is always a safe bet.

Specifics for Women's Business Casual

- *Pants/Skirts:* Women can wear casual pants or skirts. Neither should be tight. For the most business-like appearance, pants should be creased and tailored. If you are in doubt about the industry "standard", observe women in the industry on the job, at career fairs, at information sessions, etc.
- *Skirt Lengths:* Often vary from season to season. Avoid extreme trends, especially with short lengths and/or high slits. Before choosing a skirt to wear, sit down in it facing a mirror. Be critical and ask yourself if the image is a person who looks appropriate in a business environment.

- *Shirts/Sweaters:* In addition to tailored shirts, tailored knit sweaters and sweater sets are appropriate business casual choices for women.
- *Jewelry/Accessories:* Wear a conservative watch. Jewelry and scarf styles come and go. Keep your choices simple and conservative. Avoid extremes of style and color.
- *Cosmetics:* Avoid extremes of nail length and polish color, especially in conservative industries.
- *Shoes:* Shoes should be leather or micro-fiber. Regardless of style, avoid extremes. Make certain you can walk comfortably in your shoes.
- *Hose:* Hose are not essential for business casual, but are recommended with shorter skirts and in more formal environments. Trouser socks or knee-high hose are appropriate with slacks.
- *Purse/Bag:* A tailored purse is best and one that hangs on your shoulder is often advantageous as it frees your hands for greetings (handshakes) or holding a beverage. Often, leaving your purse locked in the trunk is preferable if you are uncertain what to do with it.

"Ability is what you're capable of doing. Motivation determines what you do. Attitude determines how well you do it."

— Lou Holtz
Football coach
1937-1980

"The longer I live, the more I realize the impact of attitude on life. Attitude, to me, is more important than facts. It is more important than the past, the education, the money, than circumstances, than failure, than successes, than what other people think or say or do. It is more important than appearance, giftedness or skill. It will make or break a company ... a church ... a home. The remarkable thing is we have a choice everyday regarding the attitude we will embrace for that day. We cannot change our past…we cannot change the fact that people will act in a certain way. We cannot change the inevitable. The only thing we can do is play on the one string we have, and that is our attitude. I am convinced that life is 10% what happens to me and 90% of how I react to it. And so it is with you ... we are in charge of our Attitudes."

— Charles R. Swindoll
American writer and clergyman

CHAPTER 6

ATTITUDE

A true professional is quick with a smile, has an energetic "can-do" attitude, has a positive outlook to every situation, is eager and ready to help others (especially customers), and does what needs to be done promptly on his/her own initiative.

A true professional is sensitive to co-workers, is not arrogant or short-tempered and has the ability to control and balance his/her ambition.

Attitude and Altitude

In life, our attitude determines how far and high in life we go, as well as where we go. Negative attitudes will bring to our reality negative results, in the same way that positive attitudes will bring to your reality positive results. Fix your attitude and you will be altering your circumstances.

Learning, internalizing and applying this principle will change your life forever. Start now.

85% of the Reason Someone Is Hired and Promoted

Independent research studies conducted by Harvard University and the Carnegie Organization revealed that 85% of the reason why you are hired or promoted in an organization has to do with your attitude; only 15% has to do with your skills.

At our foresight Management Development training programs, we conduct an exercise, where we ask the managers to make a list of attributes and characteristics they look in hiring a top manager for their organizations. Invariably, 85% of what they list has to do with attitudes and 15% are skills, which prove without a doubt this point.

Organizations that hire for attitude will be hiring people that will have the hunger to acquire the skills necessary to succeed in the position they have been hired for.

Consideration

A person that respects, and takes into consideration, other people's rights, feelings and well beings before they act, is always respected and liked. Consideration toward other people's rights and feelings shows respect, humility and unselfishness, all attributes of a true professional.

Unselfishness

An unselfish attitude puts other people first, over our own willpower. When we show unselfishness, we show love, respect, leadership, strength, consideration, and overall class; an attribute which is lacking in our modern society.

Courtesy

Cooperation, generosity and good manners are the characteristics of civil behavior and professionalism. When we show respect and consideration for others we show confidence and strength of character. We also show civility and good manners, becoming the kind of person our mothers wanted us to be.

Teaching and Delegation

A professional with the right attitude makes a point of teaching other people what they know. They realize that helping others to grow makes them grow also. There is an old saying: the one who teaches learns twice. As we teach and help others to grow, we reinforce the skills that we have learned and become more indispensable within our organizations.

Reacting vs. Responding

This is what I call an even attitude. Most of us tend to react to other people's input or circumstances, causing other people to resist us.

Reacting is emotional, while responding is logical. When we ask questions like, "What do you mean by that?" or, "Can you help me understand your statement?" in response to another person's reaction or criticism, you invite not resistance, but rationality, as you are asking for clarification. This technique will also give you time to think, empathize and really understand what other people are feeling and meaning, before you respond.

Positive Approach to Frustrations and Positive Expectations

Expect the best and have an attitude of gratitude, in spite of your circumstances. It is not what happens in life, but how we chose to respond to what happens, which defines our attitudes in life. Circumstances in life in reality are neutral, neither good nor bad.

Our mental attitudes and value-judgments based on past experiences and rooted assumptions are what label our circumstances as "good" or "bad". We should never surrender to our circumstances, as every circumstance is an opportunity to grow, a lesson in disguise, reveals a character flaw we have to work on or hides a future benefit.

When we learn to see life and our circumstances with hope and optimism, we become a magnet to help and lead the way for other people whom haven't learned this lesson yet.

Thoughts and Attitude Connection

Everything starts in our minds. Our most prevalent thoughts and attitudes are the builders of our habits. Our habits shape our character (who we really are). Finally, our character will determine our circumstances.

The only thing we have control over in our lives are our thoughts; we can't control people, circumstances (at least directly), or events. The only control we have is over our thoughts. Our thoughts trigger our emotions and our emotions control our behavior. Therefore, in order to change our behavior, we need to start with changing and focusing our thoughts to thoughts of goodness, joy, optimism, hope and unselfishness and of course, love...something the world could use more of.

"The fact, in short, is that freedom to be meaningful in an organized society must consist of an amalgam of hierarchy of freedoms and restraints."

— Samuel Hendel

CHAPTER 7

RESPECT FOR THE HIERARCHY OF AUTHORITY

A true professional understands structure and welcomes accountability. Therefore, a true professional is respectful and shows loyalty to the appointed chain of command and established communication channels and protocol. By showing respect to those in authority, they show their respect for themselves and set the example for others. Remember, no company will survive without order, respect and an authority hierarchy.

We all are accountable to someone else, whether to our spouses, bosses, customers, coworkers, families, friends, church pastors, parents, etc. Understanding and accepting the importance of experience and responsibility, which correspond with authority, bring efficiency and order to any organization.

Get a Promotion by Helping Promote Your Boss

The fastest way to get a promotion is not to sabotage your boss, but to help him grow and be promoted. When we become knowledgeable, necessary to the company and have a great attitude, we become candidates ourselves for promotion. If you have a boss, who in your opinion is an incompetent, don't sabotage his efforts, but become visibly more competent than him/her, as you help him/her, until it becomes so evident that a promotion will become inevitable.

Order and Team Spirit

The cliché "there is no 'I' in 'team'" is a reality that few understand. When we help other people, we encourage them to help us and to engage in their willing participation, which will help us meet our organizational goals; that's what leadership is all about. Team spirit starts with helping them achieve their goals, so they can willingly help us achieve our; it's never the other way around. When we help, cooperate, respect other people within the organization, we promote reciprocal cooperation, willingness and admiration from our peers and people we report to.

The Power of a True Leader

A true professional and leader uses the power of their authority to develop and influence people, not to feed their egos with power games or to abuse people.

The power of a true leader is based on modeling positive behaviors, developing people to realize and develop their potential and the multiplication of more leaders within the organization.

People won't resist the lines of authority if their immediate overseer is the type of person they want to become. They resist the 'jerk', the authoritarian, the egocentric, the incompetent and the elitist.

Frustrations increase within organizations, when we realize that some leaders want (and even demand) for us to follow them because of their titles. We don't respect hierarchies, we respect people.

A true professional and leader is a person that others gladly and confidently follow because he inspires respect (because he is respectful) and confidence (because he is trustworthy). Power is the ability to impose one's will on others, even if those others resist in some way. For a true professional and leader, influence is the foundation of a healthy hierarchy, not power.

"Etiquette means behaving yourself a little better than is absolutely essential."

— Will Cuppy

CHAPTER 8

PROPER BUSINESS ETIQUETTE

A true professional is always courteous, considerate, and "classy" with customers, co-workers and other people at large. "Perception is reality", therefore, rudeness on the phone, in person, or in social events creates a perception of lack of finesse (refinement) and professionalism.

Consideration and respect for other people's time is an essential aspect of business and personal etiquette. The following are some of the key business etiquette attributes true professionals must have.

Return Your Calls!

A key aspect of business etiquette and respect is to return your telephone calls, mail and e-mails promptly. Nothing sends a louder message of lack of care, disrespect and rudeness, than unanswered messages. If you say that you are going to return a call, return the call; do what you say you are going to do, when you say you are going to do it. You owe this to the customer, sales solicitors (yes, your potential suppliers) and to your company.

Many professionals return only those calls that may bring them the greatest benefit. Although this method can be a good time management tool, it lacks vision, as the sales person calling to solicit your business could be a potential customer himself, or the source of your best future customer referral. If you, out of pride or lack of sound activity management techniques, don't answer your calls (even to say thanks, but no thanks), you could be leaving a lot of money on the table.

See every caller as an opportunity, not a nuisance or an interruption, as they could hide great opportunities, which you could possibly be ignoring.

Perhaps a better technique is to spend the last hour of your day, or your most convenient time slot, answering all your calls; even the sales solicitations. Ask the sales person, while you have him/her in the phone, questions about his business and about his customers and then try to sell your own products or services to him/her; this is what the Chambers of Commerce are all about. You will find that this five minute exchange could enhance your sales by at least 5%.

Do you think 5% more in sales is worth your time? You bet it is!

Phone Etiquette

The following are other useful tips published by the College of Business of the University of Missouri in Columbia, called Telephone Etiquette 101. You can find it at http://business.missouri.edu/341/default.aspx.

For most of us, the telephone is a vital source of communication. The use of cell phones and "instant conversation" is commonplace in our life today. However, when applying for an internship or permanent position, the way you conduct yourself on the phone may be a key factor in a future customer's decision to do business with you.

Every time you talk on the phone, you represent the face of your company. The person on the other end of the phone cannot see you, so that person's first impression of you and your attitude will be determined by the tone of your voice and telephone manners.

These tips will show you how paying attention to detail may make a big difference in others impressions of you ... both personally and professionally.

Etiquette is the proper manner of conduct in any given setting. There is also a proper etiquette for telephone conversations. Always smile when you talk. Can you sense a smile? You bet! And a positive disposition on your end of the telephone line is likely to defuse grumpiness from a caller who has a complaint.

The following are some other pointers to keep in mind when you answer the telephone:

- Identify yourself, office, or organization in as few words as possible. Try as quickly as possible to learn with whom you are speaking.
- Maintain a positive and considerate attitude toward each telephone caller. A caller easily recognizes if you seem bored or anxious to get rid of them. This is discourteous and paints a poor image of you and the organization.
- Use the telephone properly. Keep your lips about one-half to 1 inch from the mouthpiece. Pronounce letters, numbers, and names clearly. Spell out names if they could be misunderstood.
- Return calls. If you must leave the telephone during a conversation and won't be able to return immediately, say that you will call back and then follow through.
- Say "good-bye" pleasantly and replace the receiver gently.
- The person making the call should always end the conversation.
- Never take phone calls while on luncheon appointments or in the middle of a meeting; have the voicemail pick your calls.

When you talk to someone in a face-to-face setting, how much of the communication message do you think is conveyed just by what you say — the words that you use? Studies show that only 7 percent of a message is conveyed through the words that you use. Another 38 percent is carried by your tone of voice. The remaining 55 percent is conveyed through body language.

Obviously, what's not available when you're on the telephone is what accounts the most: body language, and that accounts for more than half of the communication message that's conveyed. We must make up that missing 55 percent when we are on the telephone, through our voice. How do you do that?

For one, when the phone rings, be ready. Be prepared to talk. Give your attention to the caller — think of every call as a great opportunity waiting to happen. Set aside whatever you are doing and totally focus on what the caller is saying. Ask clarifying questions: "What do you mean?" or "Would you like to expand on that last point?" Periodically, paraphrase their comments so you understand what the caller means and make sure you are both in the "same page". Interact and verbally encourage the caller.

Summarize the conversation to clear up any areas of misunderstanding. Although the caller can't see them, use body gestures — body language. Gestures allow you to be more expressive, more animated in your conversation.

Also pay attention to your vocal quality, which consist of rate, pitch, volume, clarity, and tone. Is your voice rate too fast or too slow? The average speech rate is 140 words per minute. Fast talkers come across as untrustworthy or too busy to talk. Callers may think of slow talkers as mentally slow. Pitch is the highness or lowness of your voice. High-pitched talkers tend to grate on people's nerves, while low-pitched talkers sound mechanical, almost robotic; talk naturally, as you would normally speak in person. Volume is how loud or soft you talk. Loud people are perceived as brash, overbearing; soft speakers are seen as shy, wimpy. Clarity takes in how your words are understood.

Dining Manners

"It May Look Like Lunch, But It's Still Business!"

The following are some additional practical tips published by the College of Business of the University of Missouri in Columbia called Rules for Business Dining:

- When inviting a client to lunch, remember that the restaurant you select is subconsciously perceived as an extension of your office. Therefore, select a restaurant where the food is of good quality and the service is reliable.

- When escorted to a table by a Maitre d', allow your guest(s) to walk behind the person. When finding a table on your own, take the lead.
- Be sure to extend the "power" seat to your client. Seat yourself in the seat with your back facing the door/main body of the room.
- Once everyone is seated, place your napkin on your lap. This gesture serves as a cue that the meal is about to begin.
- When making a food recommendation, recognize that most guests also take your suggestion as the price range to stay within.
- When the server asks for your meal order before your guests', it's the perfect time to say, "I'd like my guest(s) to order first." Besides being appropriate, it's a cue to let the server know that the check should be left with you at the end of the meal.
- When reaching for the bread basket, salad dressing, etc., offer them to your guest(s) BEFORE using them yourself.
- Finally, tip adequately. Treat the server as one of your employees. It's a small price to pay for good service, personal attention and, hopefully, the contract that you land!

I would like to add a few more useful rules:

- Like your mother told you…never talk with your mouth full.
- Never make a promise you can't fulfill.
- Speak clearly and distinctly.
- Do not gossip.

"Knowledge comes by eyes always open and working hands; and there is no knowledge that is not power."

— Ralph Waldo Emerson
American poet, lecturer and essayist
1803-1882

CHAPTER 9

STRONG KNOWLEDGE OF YOUR COMPANY AND ITS PRODUCTS

A true professional engages in a constant quest for knowing more and more each day about the company's history, products, organization and processes. The more that a professional knows about the business he is in, the more he projects professionalism and shows command of his trade.

Also, technical competence of your company's products will turn you into a more effective problem solver and a more strategic and creative thinker.

Most people tend to learn as much as they can about their particular department (accounting, packaging, etc.) or line of work, ignoring other functions and areas of operations. I call that attitude insular (inward-focused) thinking.

When we go outside of our area of work to study as much as we can, the functions and processes of other departments, the functions of different people within the organization, competitive products, the future and direction of the industry; that's what I call open-minded professionalism.

Don't Be Afraid To Ask Questions; Be Curious

Be a student of your company's products, your competition

and the industry you are in. Ask questions to your senior management, search the Web, download or order catalogs and brochures from competitive companies, and research trade associations for training opportunities within your industry or line of work.

Be a "sponge", absorbing everything you can and learning everything that there is to learn. Learn how the products are made, different manufacturing techniques and processes, distribution channels; how your competitors are marketing and advertising their products; how your competitor's websites look; find out about their pricing, merchandising, and promotions.

If you limit your scope of knowledge and training only in the area of the company you are working, you won't be able to advance too fast in other areas of the company when the opportunity knocks at your door. Many of the most successful CEOs of major companies have started from the bottom working their way up, by showing an attitude of eagerness to learn all that there is to learn, even if they don't have to or are asked to.

By being a student of your company and your field you will become more creative, resourceful and useful in your workplace. Leaders pay attention to people within their organizations who show an attitude of learning, growing and inquisitive minds.

Always find and make time for growing through learning, researching, training and mentoring other people. Throughout my career, I have met many managers who never seem to have time for training, reading or growing. Those are the people who, at the end, will spend a tremendous amount of time just keeping things as they are, or innovating very little because they haven't mastered the skill of finding the time to transform themselves, in order to be able to transform their organizations.

The more that you know about your company, its products, its competitors and the industry, the more essential, relevant and trustworthy you become within your company.

"For every minute spent in organizing, an hour is earned."
— Unknown

CHAPTER 10

PERSONAL ORGANIZATION SKILLS

A true professional knows the importance of personal and professional organization and discipline, in order to be more productive, accurate in his work and to have the ability to meet deadlines and appointments (a quality that is very much respected by other professionals).

He/she recognizes the value, thus, practice the skill of working smarter and faster.

Clean vs. Cluttered Work Area

A cluttered work area is a reflection of a cluttered mind. A clean, uncluttered work space keeps your mind focused and will make you more productive. If we spend five minutes every hour trying to locate lost files, papers, etc. it represent thirteen hours a month of lost productivity.

When our work areas are disorganized and cluttered, we tend to wander around and have disorganized thoughts.

Have a Designated Place for Everything

My father used to say: "there is a place for everything and everything has a place"; he was right. Organize your workspace making sure that everything has a designated place. There is a vast array of storage products and office organizers to meet any need at your local office supplies store. The goal is to have everything organized in trays, storage boxes, files, etc., so you can unclutter the desk and other workspaces.

Make a habit to file or store on a daily basis, classifying every document, letter, file, etc. in its designated space, out of sight, as they come to you.

Set a Specific Daily Time to Read

For a true professional, reading, whether it is a professional magazine, professional or self-help books or reports, it is important to keep ourselves relevant and updated. Choose a time of day where you are not tired from a long day of work for your reading. Use a well light area, so you won't strain your eyes. Make reading an important part of your life and your habits. One of the fastest and cheapest ways of learning is by reading.

Browse Magazines; Cut the Articles You Want to Read and Trash the Rest

When you receive professional magazines, browse it for the articles you want to read, clip out the pages and file them in a folder for reading during your designated reading time. This practice not only helps you focus on your reading, but helps you stay organized, avoid procrastination, as well as keeps magazines out of sight and reduces clutter in your workspace.

Use of a Label Printer

One of the tools I have found most useful is a label printer. A label printer provides for a fast, easy way to print file folder labels. By using a label printer, I avoid procrastinating in opening a new file. I just print the label, stick it to a folder and get the document out of my sight by creating a "home" for each and every document I have on my desk.

Contact Management Software

One of the most effective personal and professional organization tools is the use of contact management software such as ACT or GoldMine, among others. With good contact management

software you can:
1. Schedule appointments.
2. Keep detailed notes of conversations with customers.
3. Keep all your contacts' information in a database you can access in many different ways.
4. Keep TO DO lists and track your work performed and work pending.
5. With a contact management software, you can send faxes, e-mails, proposals and correspondence, all attached to your contact person's electronic file.
6. Send marketing e-mails.
7. Use alarms and reminders for your programmed activities.

I have used ACT for many years. It is very intuitive and easy to use and I assure you, it will become your best ally in customer service and customer relationships; as well as, one of your most valuable time management tools.

"Time is free, but it's priceless. You can't own it, but you can use it. You can't keep it, but you can spend it. Once you've lost it you can never get it back."

— Harvey MacKay

CHAPTER 11

SHARPENING YOUR TIME MANAGEMENT SKILLS

As time management experts say, the paradox of time management is that we can't manage time, we can only manage our activities. For a true professional, the wise and efficient use of time is essential to accomplish goals, enjoy life and have an overall healthy and balanced life.

Get Organized!

The first step to manage your activities is to identify your time wasters and interruptions. Use a calendar to record for one full week your current activities, day by day, hour by hour.

The second most important step is to organize yourself in a way where everything on top of your desk now has a place which is very handy and easy to find. Among the ideas you may want to consider are:

1. File every important document you need for future reference. Use a small label printer to create labels fast and with ease.
2. Use a tray to file all your documents that require action and label it "TO DO".
3. Without rationalizing, trash everything else.

4. Don't allow any interruptions while you are getting organized; totally focus on the task at hand until you finish. Otherwise, you will procrastinate and you will never get it done.
5. Use a three-ring binder with dividers. Open a section on a master paper to write down all the notes hanging around your walls on sticky notes.
6. In another section of the three-ring binder write a master list of all your pending projects and items that need follow up in the form of a TO DO list.
7. Cut the articles of interest in all the magazines, newspapers and periodicals and open a reading file and label it: TO READ. Trash the rest.
8. Clean your drawers, tossing everything that you haven't used in 18 months, or at least store it in a supply cabinet or storage room. Out of sight...but organized.
9. Review your briefcase taking out all the papers, letters etc. Take the contents and file them, place them in your TO DO tray, or trash them accordingly.
10. To stay organized, before you leave for the day, clean and organize your desk, using the above tips.

The Law of the Vital Few and the Trivial Many

In 1906, Italian economist, Vilfredo Pareto created a mathematical formula to describe the unequal distribution of wealth in his country, Italy. He observed that twenty percent of the people owned eighty percent of the wealth and realized that the same phenomena applied to many other disciplines as well.

The famous Pareto Principle proposes that 80% of the effects come from 20% of the causes. In other words, 20% of the essentials always accounts for 80% of the results. The key is to find out the 20% of activities that really matters and that produces 80% of the most significant results.

In Pareto's case it meant 20 percent of the people owned 80 percent of the wealth. Dr. Joseph Juran, a pioneer in quality management, stated that 20 percent of the defects were causing 80 percent of the problems. Project Managers recognize that 20 percent of the work takes up 80 percent of your time and resources. You can apply the 80/20 Rule to almost anything, from sales to management to physics.

The value of the Pareto Principle for a manager is that it helps you realize and focus on the 20 percent that really matters. Of everything you do during your day, only 20 percent really matters. That 20 percent produces 80 percent of your results. The key is to identify and focus on those things.

To identify your 20% vital few:

1. Make a list of those things at work that are absolutely crucial; they must get done.
2. Classify the list and find out how many of those activities contribute to increase sales, profit, employee development or product development.
3. If something in the schedule has to be pushed, if something isn't going to get done, make sure it's not part of that 20 percent.

Be Discriminate With Time Spent On Web Searches

Web surfing could be one of the most powerful time wasters in your work day. Web searches may not only be unethical, if it is not work related, but sometimes it consumes an enormous amount of time, as we get distracted surfing from one site to the next. If you must do Web searches as part of your job, leave them for the end of the day, when you can do it uninterrupted. You will find that you will be more focused and efficient, as you have a self-imposed time limit, in order to go home.

Productive Meetings

In order to keep meetings productive, short and to the point, the following tips may be helpful:

1. Clearly define the goal of the meeting.
2. Write and circulate an agenda in advance, requesting the

documents, reports, ideas, etc. you want them to bring to the meeting. Define the amount of time each person will have on the agenda. Always allow sufficient time for preparation.

3. Use a recorder to prepare a post-meeting follow up list and to keep minutes of the meeting. Circulate the minutes with the follow up points to all the participants.

Use of Daily Planners

Use a daily planner to record all your activities for the day, which may be classified as:

1. **To Do**
2. **Appointments**
3. **Calls**
4. **Special Projects**

If you are using an electronic planner (recommended) such as ACT, Palm, or Outlook, make sure to use the activity alarms, to alert you ahead of time when you need to make a call or leave for a meeting. Usually, a common reason why we get to appointments late is because we don't allow ourselves enough time to quit office work and get ourselves on the road for a scheduled meeting.

Also, make sure you use the feature that automatically transfers today's undone TO DO's for tomorrow.

Procrastination

Procrastination is defined as putting off intentionally the doing of something that should be done today. Intentionally putting off something that should be done has its roots in fear. Two of the main reasons why we put off things for which we know we need to do today are:

- Perfectionism-we want to make sure that all the perfect conditions are there before we start our project (yeah, right).
- Lack of Knowledge (insecurity)- When we don't know or feel insecure on how to do something, we tend to wait until we receive "divine revelation" before we start, rather than research and look for the necessary information that will teach us how to do it.

As a habit, procrastination can be a major obstacle in both your career and your personal life. Procrastination is the cause of many missed opportunities, frantic work hours at the "last minute", which causes stress and a sense of feeling overwhelmed, which escalates into resentment, guilt and anger; all negative emotions you can avoid.

When you think of something you have to do as a "big" project which will take up a lot of time, you will certainly put it off. Think of a project as a number of smaller pieces that go together like a puzzle (tasks). Then, address each task, one at a time, a bite at a time, rather than trying to swallow the whole chunk.

Replace the "must do" thinking with an "I'll do" attitude. "Must" implies that you are "forced" to do it, as if it were a duty and not a choice, therefore, you will automatically feel a sense of heaviness, resentment and a desire to do it "later", when you feel more motivated to do it. An "I'll do" attitude sends a clear message to your subconscious mind that you are choosing to do it and that you will be successful at it. It implies that you are in control of the project, rather than the project having control over you.

A common faulty thinking that leads to procrastination is perfectionism, which is the thinking that says that all the circumstances have to be "right", in order to be able to do the job perfectly. Obviously, the "perfect" set of circumstances doesn't show, therefore, we talk ourselves out of starting what we know we should do anyway.

Believing that you must do something perfectly is a cause for major stress, which becomes a vicious cycle, because you associate that stress with the task, thus you talk yourself into avoidance until the very last minute.

If we don't set a specific deadline for a task or a project, perfectionism and procrastination will cause us to delay indefinitely. Therefore, always set up realistic completion dates for each task and each project.

Another faulty thinking is the mental association that the time you spend undertaking a task or a project will take away from the "fun stuff", the life's pleasures (like watching TV, working on a hobby, resting, etc.). When you feel this way, do both; combine business with pleasure. Work on a task until completion. Then, reward yourself with a pleasure (like going to the movies).

Then repeat the process until the project is done. Schedule ahead of time the time you will allocate each week to family time, entertainment, exercise, social activities, and personal hobbies and all your favorite leisure activities. Work your projects in small bites and reward yourself after each completion.

Another technique is to allocate a certain amount of time (say, two to four hours at a time) to start and finish more than one task; then reward yourself. Knowing that you have to wait only a few hours before you get the reward, helps you keep going, as you know you can enjoy the reward whenever you have finished the task.

By rewarding yourself for simply putting in the time, instead of for any specific achievements, you'll be eager to return to work on your task over and over again, until you finish the project.

Overcoming procrastination is about reducing the mental associations of pain and increase the mental associations of pleasure and accomplishment when beginning a task, thus gradually eliminating the inertia created by your old faulty thoughts.

"Self-discipline begins with the mastery of your thoughts. If you don't control what you think, you can't control what you do. Simply, self-discipline enables you to think first and act afterward."
— Napoleon Hill
American author, 1883-1970

"Discipline is the bridge between goals and accomplishment."
— Jim Rohn
American speaker and author
Famous for motivational audio programs for business and life

CHAPTER 12

DISCIPLINE

Discipline is defined as the control we gain by applying orderly conduct or exercising a pattern of behavior, which perfects good habits, moral character and our mental faculties.

A true professional exercises his/her determination to choose self-discipline, self-control, self-regulation, self-restraint, and self-imposed order, which constitute the only path toward the achievement of any personal or professional goal. Self-discipline is control over our own weaknesses, temptations, impulses and emotions. It comes with the practice of determination, persistence, patience, restraint and endurance.

Our habits make us or destroy us and the control of our thoughts is the springboard that forms our habits. By taming our thoughts, we master our habits. Only by repetition and persistence we are able to develop good habits, which will shape and determine our circumstances.

Winners do what losers don't like to do. The development of discipline is one of those things losers don't like to do. A habit is a choice that we repeat until it becomes comfortable and part of us.

In the same way we teach our children discipline by forcing them to do what they naturally don't want to do, we have to force ourselves to do those things that we naturally don't like to do.

Discipline is self-control. It is setting limits and correcting unhealthy behavior.

When we focus our thoughts and dwell on the benefit that modifying our behavior will bring, it will become easier for us to follow through and to persevere until we have mastered and conquered our habits.

With your first success in practicing self-discipline, a renewed surge of enthusiasm will propel you to the realization of your next goal in habit formation.

By exercising self-discipline, we can overcome addictions, eliminate procrastination, or overcome ignorance and poverty. Discipline is something that we develop gradually, with persistence, focus, repetition and by never giving up.

When we were kids and wanted to learn how to ride a bicycle, we started by having a burning desire. Then we started practicing with easier, less challenging task: training wheels (undertake easier tasks where you feel confident to succeed). After we were comfortable, and we wanted to be like the "big kids", we tried increasing the challenge by lifting the training wheels (increased the challenge). We practiced with enthusiasm every day (repetition and perseverance).

Soon enough, we would remove the wheels and fly (success!). As we practiced some more, we started practicing tricks, like "look mama no hands" (confidence encouraged more confidence and mastery).

The principles on developing discipline are no different than the bicycle example above; in fact, you have already successfully practiced self-discipline before, and if you apply the principle, you can conquer self-discipline and master whatever you want in life.

As you develop self-discipline, never compare yourself with others. Pride is comparing our strength with other's weakness and weakness is comparing ourselves with others we perceive are stronger. If you think you're weak, everyone else will seem stronger. If you think you're strong, everyone else will seem weaker; that's human nature.

Set your own personal goals and compare yourself only in relation to your goals and what you can still accomplish. Assess and accept realistically your present reality. If you want to lose 30 pounds, start with accepting your present weight and work a plan (disciplined diet and disciplined exercising) to realistically lose two to three pounds per week. Don't focus on the 30 pounds you want to lose, just focus on the two or three pounds you will be losing this week. Soon enough, you would have lost 30 pounds with a minimum of frustration (see chapter 11 on procrastination).

Developing discipline is like body building or exercising, we need a plan, we need to train progressively and consistently, we need to work hard, and we must persevere and never give up.

The process of self-discipline involves willpower, which is another word for determination. We must be sure of what we want and be determined to pay the price to make it come through.

Determination is about deciding, definitely and firmly; it is the power or habit to choose to do something definitely and firmly, without hesitation; like the shoemaker, Nike, says: Just do it!

Determination is what ignites and propels the process of self-discipline and what takes you to the starting point. It is what breaks the inertia and stops procrastination.

Discipline involves doing your work with intensity and persistence. Determination and persistence develop discipline; and sustained discipline develops endurance, or staying power. Self-discipline requires that you develop the capacity to put in the effort and the time where it's needed.

When you discipline yourself to do what seems hard, and what you don't feel like doing, but are required to do, you gain the strength denied to undisciplined people. The determination to do what seems difficult in order to meet a worthy goal is the same principle required to search for gold or diamonds; it is like having a key to a special treasure chest.

Being industrious is putting steady, habitual effort and diligence, as well as the time necessary to pursue and reach a goal. Disciplining yourself to be industrious allows you to squeeze more productivity out of your time. Time is invariable and fixed; your personal productivity is the only thing you can increase or decrease.

Persistence

Sticking to the task ahead when everyone else is ready to quit is the mark of a persistent professional. Many people abandon a task at the first signs of resistance, failure or complications. That is why a persistent individual stands out over the crowd. Always look for different ways to accomplish and address a difficult task and don't quit until you achieve the ultimate goal. Remember that a quitter never wins and a winner never quits!

No human quality is more important in the accomplishment of any endeavor than persistence. My favorite definition of persistence is the ability to maintain action regardless of your feelings. You press on even when you feel like quitting. Persistence allows you to keep taking action when you don't feel motivated to do so, and thus, you keep achieving results, which supplies and fuel more motivation.

Calvin Coolidge, the 30th President of the United States, eloquently said, "Nothing in the world can take the place of persistence. Talent will not; nothing is more common than unsuccessful men with talent. Genius will not; unrewarded genius is almost a proverb. Education will not; the world is full of educated derelicts. Persistence and determination alone are omnipotent. The slogan "Press On" has solved and always will solve the problems of the human race." Amen!

Persistence doesn't mean that you keep doing things that don't work, blindly and stubbornly. Albert Einstein's definition of insanity is to "do the same thing, the same way, over and over, expecting a different result." Therefore, we should always be applying, adjusting, changing and reviewing our plans, strategy and tactics and timelines. What must stay unchanged is the goal, not the tactics to achieve the goal.

"By constant self-discipline and self-control you can develop greatness of character."

— Grenville Kleiser
American author 1868-1953

CHAPTER 13

SELF-CONTROL

A true professional and leader chooses control over anger; chooses to respond, rather than to react; chooses to think, before taking action or rushing into judgments. A true professional postpones judgment until he/she can gather the facts. Leaders always praise in public and reprimand in private.

Make the habit of letting letters and e-mails of a sensitive nature rest for 24 hours, before you send them. You will find that a letter that you write today contains many emotions that you may find offensive tomorrow. Remember that once you put the letter in the mailbox or push the "send" button on your computer, you will not be able to take back what you said. Many relationships are irreparably broken for dealing with people out of emotional reactions, rather than out of rational, well thought-out communication.

As I mentioned before, we can't control people or events, but we can exercise control over our own emotions, if we only allow ourselves the discipline to do so.

The first step for developing self-control is to identify those areas where you feel out of control. That could be anger, eating or drinking habits, addictions, lying, people pleasing, or overworking (workaholics).

Second, identify the emotions that make you more vulnerable

and lead you to feel out of control.

Third, examine your self-talk process leading to your lack of self-control.

Fourth, develop new self-talk, this time rationalizing your behavior and encouraging yourself in your efforts at developing self-control ("I will not get angry with him/her; I chose to think and respond, instead of reacting.")

Fifth, develop and write down a self-talk statement for each item you want to gain control over (see first step), so you can use it every time lack of self-control emerges.

Sixth, prioritize the issues that need more prompt attention in the lack of self-control department. Start working first with the ones that need more attention, which are the ones that affect other people the most.

Seventh, practice, practice, practice until you master it.

And remember that the old technique of counting to ten while taking a couple of deep breaths before responding, is as valid now as it has ever been; use it, it works!

Don't get discouraged if you start practicing self-discipline and you fail. As you practice the discipline of self-control, you will find yourself, at times, failing. Remember, it's going to be hard at the beginning because your old set of rooted beliefs will be resisting the new programming. As in any endeavor in life, practice creates the habit and once you have the habit, becoming self-controlled is just a step away.

In order to see yourself achieving the success you desire in life: success in your personal life or your professional life, you must have self control. It is first a choice and then an action. Apply each step of the process for developing self-control, and see yourself succeeding. You choose to win the battle over self!

"Communication is a skill that you can learn. It's like riding a bicycle or typing. If you're willing to work at it, you can rapidly improve the quality of every part of your life."

— Brian Tracy
Author, Lecturer and American television host

CHAPTER 14

GOOD COMMUNICATION AND PRESENTATION SKILLS

Of all the attributes a true professional must have in their toolbox, communication tops the list. We spend 85% or more of our awake time communicating in one way or another. We need good communications skills to connect with our spouses, our children, bosses, employees, customers, friends, etc.

A true professional learns to know him/herself and to know other people better, in order to have the ability to communicate and present ideas effectively.

Listening

1. Give your total concentration and attention to the speaker. Show that you care by putting-off all other activities, physically or mentally.

2. Show the speaker that you understand what he/she is saying by using verbal replies (like "I understand"; "Really"; "I see") and nonverbally (with nods, expressing interest). Lean toward the speaker and make constant eye contact. Speak at about the same voice level as the other person.

3. Show that you understand what has been said by occasionally rephrasing the substance of their thought or by asking a

question which shows you know the thought being expressed. Do not constantly repeat what they've said to prove you were listening, but to show you understand what he/she is saying. The difference in these two intents communicates remarkably different messages to the speaker.

4. Show the speaker respect. You do this by communicating with the speaker at their level of understanding and attitude by adjusting your tone of voice, rate of speech, and choice of words to show that you feel sympathy, understanding and compassion for what they are saying.

Critical Dialogues

Many important conversations pop up without warning and at the least expected moments. These conversations can range from an exchange where bets are high, (like in certain negotiations); or where opinions are different than ours (our idea vs. someone else's idea) and/or emotions are strong (an irate customer is shouting his complaint).

Some people typically handle these conversations by (1) avoiding them; and (2) by handling them poorly because they catch them off-balance. You can handle them well if you practice a few rules which will give you the leading edge. These rules are:

1. Be Empathic (understanding, compassionate, supportive)
   - Restate (paraphrase) what you heard the customer say.
   - Ask questions. Make the customer feel valued.
   - Mirror — increase safety by respectfully acknowledging the emotions people appear to be feeling.
2. Be Responsive and Proactive
   - Agree — on every important point, say so and move on; don't turn an agreement into an argument.
   - Build — say things such as "Absolutely…In addition, I noticed that…"; then, add elements that were left out of the discussion.
   - Compare — when you differ. "I think I see things

differently. Let me describe how."
3. Be Competent
    - When a customer brings a problem to our attention, immediately take ownership of the problem and think about a creative solution to the problem, then, tell them how you are going to resolve it.

Basic Guidelines for Designing Your Presentation

Whether you are making a sales presentation, a presentation of an idea, a budget, a business or marketing plan or a major speech to an audience, there is a lot that can be quickly gained or quickly lost from a presentation. A little bit of skill and a lot of practice will go a long way toward making a highly effective presentation.

Organization of the Presentation

1. List the top three goals that you want to accomplish with your audience. Make sure that the points you want to present to your audience (of one, or one hundred people) are completely clear and meet each of the goals you want to accomplish. It could be, and very often is, very easy for your audience to completely miss the point of your presentation for lack of focus. For example, your goals may be for them to appreciate the quality and features of your new products, learn how to use them, etc. Again, the goals are listed based on what you want to accomplish with your audience.

2. Clearly define who your audience is and why it is important for them to be in the presentation. Your audience will want to know right away why they were the ones invited to be in your presentation. Be sure that your presentation makes this clear to them right away. This will help you clarify your invitation list and design your invitation to them.

3. List the major points of information that you want to convey to your audience. When you're done making that list, ask yourself, "If everyone in the audience understands all of those points; will I have achieved the goal that I set for this meeting?"

4. Be clear about the voice pitch and mood and emotions that you want to convey for your presentation; for example: hopefulness, enthusiasm, seriousness, celebration, humor, warning, etc. Consciously identifying the tone you want to convey can help you project that mood to your audience.

5. Design a brief opening (about 5-10% of your total presentation time) that:
   - Present your goals for the presentation.
   - Clarify the benefits of the presentation to the audience.
   - Explain the overall layout of your presentation.

6. Develop the content and organization of your presentation (about 70-80% of your presentation time).

7. Prepare a brief closing (about 5-10% of your presentation time) that summarizes the key points from your presentation.

8. Design time for questions and answers (about 10% of the time of your presentation).

Delivery Guidelines

1. If you're speaking to a small group (for example, 2-15 people), then try to accomplish eye contact with each person for a few seconds throughout your delivery.

2. Prepare an outline from your presentation in font size 20, glancing at it every 5-10 seconds; but keep an eye most of the time on your audience.

3. Speak a little bit louder and a little bit slower than you normally would do with a friend. A good way to practice these guidelines is to speak along with a news anchor when you're watching television.

4. Adjust the volume and rate of your speech and gestures to the size of your audience and age group. Lots of energy and hand gestures will work better with a younger audience; a more sober, but enthusiastic tone will work better with more mature audiences. Always remember that a monotone voice is absolutely poisonous for keeping the attention of an

audience.

5. Stand with your feet at shoulder-length apart.

In daily communications, the expansion of the vocabulary we choose is crucial to your success as a professional. Avoid offensive slang, or street (foul) language and cursing at all cost. Street language doesn't show toughness or that you are "in", but rather weakness and a limited vocabulary. If you use street language, people will perceive you and treat you according to such a level. Therefore, the first step to good communication is to improve your vocabulary, including your technical vocabulary of your industry or profession. Make a commitment to look in the dictionary and learn a new word every day.

Written Communications

The following tips can help you navigate in the world of written communications:

1. Be clear about your goal and communicate it in a short and concise manner. You must define what the goal of the communication is, as well as what is what you are trying to achieve, for example:
   - What is the purpose of the written communication?
   - What is the specific action you want the person to take?
2. Answer the five "Ws" used in journalism to tell the story: Who, what, where, when and how.
3. Capture the reader's attention on the first sentence of the first paragraph.
4. Use familiar words and phrases; familiar to the industry and familiar in the English language.
5. Mention the reader's name and his company throughout the letter.
6. Avoid too many "I's" in the letter or avoid it altogether if possible.
7. Use a conversational style.
8. Explain what you want the person receiving it to do.

- Is it to explain or clarify something?
- Are you just sharing information, or do you want a specific reply from the receiving person?

9. Explain the benefits for responding as requested.
10. Always provide an encouragement or benefit for the reader to respond back to your communication.
11. Avoid giving the reader deadlines for the response (which may sound like an ultimatum), unless it is so required by the circumstances or for legal purposes. Rather use something like "I would appreciate your prompt response."
12. Establish credibility and show respect for the reader.
13. In any written communication, be very careful about spelling, grammar and punctuation. Typos are much more tolerated in e-mail messages than in business letters, because people usually understand they are written quickly. However, be aware that many people are offended by sloppiness, so always re-read your message before sending it, or better yet, let it sit for 24-hours and re-read it again before sending it. With this discipline, you may be able to separate and eliminate harmful emotions that you didn't see the first time around, thus saving yourself a lot of grief and embarrassment. Spell-check your e-mail before sending them is always a wise choice.
14. Always show respectful attitudes and language in your communications.
15. Choose an appropriate communication method.
16. Have someone else do a quick edit and proofread your letter or report.
17. E-mail is quickly replacing formal business letters in many situations because of the faster turnaround time. But e-mails are a more informal type of communication and are no substitute to formal communications.
18. When writing to strangers, the techniques described above apply but formal business letters are more appropriate.

E-mail is more adequate between people who already have an established relationship. However, when writing to someone you don't know, we suggest taking the time to write a formal business letter for greater effectiveness.

"Temperance is moderation in the things that are good and total abstinence from the things that are foul."
— Frances E. Willard

"Temperance is simply a disposition of the mind which binds the passions."
— St. Thomas Aquinas
Scholastic philosopher and theologian
1225-1274

CHAPTER 15

TEMPERANCE

Temperance is moderation in action. It is the restraint of indulging in appetites or passions. It is the abstinence from the use of anything that alters our state of mind, such as drugs and alcohol. It is also the control of your anger, your sexual desire outside marriage, your greed and your carnal obsession and impulses for self-gratification, such as obsessive compulsive eating.

Intemperance governs over your appetites for pleasure, while temperance is your own rational control over your unhealthy appetites; it is the conscious reprogramming of rooted assumptions and beliefs, substituting them for a new truth of good and healthy habits.

The good habit (virtue) of temperance requires that you prepare and train yourself even when you are not faced with an immediate temptation. Again, it all starts with taming your thoughts through disciplined thinking. A true professional is required to develop the habit of moderation and is expected to have control over their desire for pleasure and self-gratification.

A lack of moderation undermines discretion, and if discretion and trust are destroyed, all the other virtues or good habits are undermined.

Moderation itself needs to be nurtured, and this is part of the responsibility of culture. In our modern society, you are constantly bombarded by images and messages of self-indulgence that appeal to your senses. The more you are exposed to these messages the more your judgment is undermined and you get convinced that self-indulgence is the portal to "happiness".

The culture, with its selfish consumption messages, directly reflects in the way you speak and act as well. A culture of lust and intemperance says, "I want it and I want it now." A culture of moderation and temperance says, "I can wait and delay the gratification for my own good," or "this is not good for me, even if it looks like fun."

A good way to practice temperance is to think of the consequence of your intemperate act, before acting on it. Instead of indulging in the faulty thinking that an intemperate action will bring you pleasure, analyze in a rational way and meditate on the negative consequences of the intemperate act. As you engage in this rational thinking, you will start losing the desire for intemperance, as you realize that the consequence and impact of intemperance in your life is a lot harsher, negative and detrimental than the short term artificial gratification you think you will experience by acting intemperance; it boils down to a choice.

Intemperance comes to your life through your most prevalent thoughts and it will be tamed also by your most prevalent thoughts. Your most prevalent thoughts will become your habits; your habits shape your character and your character determines your circumstances.

Your character (who you are when you are alone in front of a mirror) determines your current circumstances or what happens in your life. Your life and circumstances are the sum total of your choices (good or bad). It is like a checking account: your balance is equal to the deposits you make (good, unselfish choices) less the withdrawals you make (bad or selfish choices).

If you want to control your intemperate habits, guard your mind, as your thoughts are the roots which control and feed your actions.

Choosing the right attitude, the right thought and the right action in any circumstance requires you to develop thoughts of success and achievement as a habit of thought. Consequences are the result of choices, and those choices must include tempering your actions and your thoughts.

Bottom line, temperance versus intemperance forces you to ask yourself what choices will you make and what character will you choose to display.

"There is a magnet in your heart that will attract true friends. That magnet is unselfishness, thinking of others first…when you learn to live for others, they will live for you."
— Paramahansa Yogananda

"Real unselfishness consists in sharing the interests of others."
— George Santayana
Spanish-born American philosopher, poet and humanist
1863-1952

Chapter 16

Unselfishness

Let's face it; man is essentially selfish by nature. Let me prove my point. If we have in front of us two choices, we will choose the one that is better for us. Not the one that is better for humanity or the one that is better for my neighbor; but it is human nature that we will choose the option that is better for us.

We may have chosen an option that benefits, say, your company, but if you trace your motives, you will discover that although it benefits your company, ultimately, it will benefit you and that was the real hidden motive of why you made the choice, and not out of an unselfish virtue.

We may give someone a gift, because later on we will ask for a favor that will benefit us. We may send a note of encouragement to someone, in order to maintain our reputation of being an encourager…or just to be loved. And so it goes on and on.

People have a tendency act in ways they believe will make themselves "happy" or will remove discomfort from their life. Because we are all different from everyone else, each individual goes about feeling good about him/herself or about life in general in his own particular way. In every case, the ultimate motivation is the same: to be "happy". What varies between them is the definition and the means each has chosen to define and gain this happiness.

You either choose to seek happiness through "selfish" actions, or through "unselfish" actions. Both the crook and the humanitarian have the same motive — to do what he/she believes will make him/her feel "good." The truth is that, since Adam and Eve in the Garden of Eden, we can conclude that everyone is selfish; it's just a matter of degree.

Today, selfishness is not perceived as a major issue in our society and culture, because everyone selfishly seeks their own happiness as they constantly pursue their own interests.

The reality is that this would be a much better world if we would choose to work for the benefit of others. In fact, we could all find the much sought-after identity and true happiness, if we just choose to be giving, unselfish, sharing, helpful, and caring. We teach it to our children, but the truth is that many times we don't practice it ourselves.

As I say in my book, *Are You the Architect of Your Circumstances?* "The world does not favor the greedy, the dishonest, the vicious, although on the mere surface it may sometimes appear to do so; it admires and helps the honest, the magnanimous, the righteous." All the great teachers of the ages have declared this in different ways.

If we pursue professionalism, we must pursue and practice unselfishness. This is a key attribute that is essential to professionals.

Do you want to enrich someone's life? Go for it — use your talents, insight and generosity to give riches of happiness to the one person(s) God has entrusted and placed within your life. I guarantee that you'll have more genuine personal fulfillment, as you discover the gift of enriching others in your life.

Unselfishness will make you a better leader, a better manager, a better father, a better husband, a better son, a better brother/sister, a better … need I say more?

"Who is too old to learn is too old to teach."

— Proverb

"We accomplish all that we do through delegation — either to time or to other people."

— Stephen R. Covey

CHAPTER 17

ABILITY AND DISPOSITION TO TRAIN THROUGH DELEGATION

Training and mentoring other people is an unselfish act (if you do it for the right motives). A true professional is eager and open at all times to teach someone else what they know. The more that you teach, the more that you learn; the more that you learn the more that you have the obligation to teach others in return.

A true professional must have the ability and disposition to train people through delegating relevant work. He accepts and champions other people's ideas and promotes teamwork.

Delegation is multiplication. When you delegate, you are freeing up your time to work on projects that can have more financial, product or people impact in your organization. When you delegate, you are developing other people's skills and capabilities. People will feel valued and trusted by you. New ideas and the ownership of such ideas are more likely to be generated when other people are involved in the work.

Delegation also means letting go of control and of the thinking that no one can do the job better than you do. Mistakes are a great learning vehicle and a key developmental tool. Delegation is good and benefits everyone. Sometimes you may have to lower your own perfectionist standards and let people find their own solutions and ways of doing things.

Delegation is also the opportunity to give people the mentoring, teaching and guidance they need to learn and accomplish the job, thereby, developing more valuable members for your team.

The secondary, but obvious, benefit is that you will no longer be up to your neck in pending work. Delegation is a key management skill that, when practiced, will benefit the whole organization.

Delegation has five key components:

1. Review the project or task, as well as the desired end result, with the person you are delegating.
2. Give them the authority to execute and the grace to make mistakes.
3. Negotiate and agree on the timetable and inspection points; along with when you will be making progress reviews of the project or delegated task.
4. Assure them that you are unconditionally available for help (and mean it).
5. Without being overwhelming or controlling, look over the progress (see #3).

Delegation is about directing the growth of people. It is about improving the core skills and knowledge of people, in order to stay ahead of evolving trends and to improve the quality and quantity of our management teams. This effort can take place internally from people with more experience and knowledge within the organization, or externally by specialized companies with the appropriate expertise.

The internal effort, or mentoring (a trusted counselor or guide), should be a continuous responsibility and effort of the true professional. He/she should be in constant watch, trying to identify developmental needs they can offer to teach among peers and subordinates.

Every company should have a cross-training program. This is when you are fully trained in more than one position of responsibility, so you can create the flexibility and productivity improvement, whereas everyone knows how to perform and can cover for everyone else's positions. As true professionals you should ask to be cross-trained and you should offer to be part of the teaching process.

"The customer is our reason for being here."
— Unknown

"When the customer comes first, the customer will last."
— Robert Half

"If you work just for money, you'll never make it, but if you love what you're doing and you always put the customer first, success will be yours."
— Ray Kroc
American pioneer of the fast-food industry, founder of McDonald's
1902-1984

CHAPTER 18

CUSTOMER SATISFACTION ATTITUDE

A true professional chooses to have a positive "can do-will do" attitude that separates the winners from the losers. True professionals have learned that their first loyalty is with their company; but their first duty is to the company's customers. Without satisfied, loyal customers buying from your company time and time again, your company has no future, thus, you'll have no future.

It's difficult to think of any kind of business that doesn't live or die by its customer focus. As a true professional, you have to go from just decent service to exceptional customer service if you want to stand out.

The first step of taking the challenge of becoming exceptional in your customer service skills is the motivation to serve and help others (which goes back to chapter #16 on unselfishness). You have to take personal ownership and constantly remember that a customer's problem is your problem.

The second step is to be flexible, as each customer has and offers a different challenge. You have to become an expert at "plan Bs" (adapting to whatever comes your way, by seeking creative alternative solutions).

The third step is to be enthusiastic and energetic at the point of contact with a customer. People love to deal with positive, enthusiastic people and are put-off by low energy, unenthusiastic people. When a customer is not happy and gets in touch with a company with enthusiastic "can-do" attitude professionals, it tends to defuse the customer's negative attitude toward the company and they become a partner in the problem solving process.

The fourth step is to take ownership of your customer's situation or problem. When they call, you have to make sure that once they share their problem, automatically it becomes yours and you are going to look for a way to solve it, beyond the customer's expectations, and then some. You have to make them feel as if you are part of their team (as you really are).

Finally, as Lisa Ford, one of the foremost customer service authority in the world, says, "Be consistent (do what you say that you are going to do, when you say you are going to do it, all the time) and be creative in serving your customer and love what you do."

The following statistics will help show the importance and financial impact of exceptional customer service. In his book, The Loyalty Effect, Frederick Reichheld tells us, based on his research work, that if we can keep 5% more of our existing customers every year we can boost profits by 25-125%, depending on the industry. He also says that if we keep just 2% more of our customers, it has the same financial impact on profits as cutting costs by 10%. Apply these numbers to your particular company situation and be surprised by how much money is at stake!

Survey studies also show that 40% of the reason why customers switch to a competitor is due to poor service and only 8% said it was because of cost. No wonder why customer service beyond expectations is not an option if you want to stay in business.

The lesson learned here is that when running a business all things must be considered, even the often times-overlooked things like customer service. Besides the profit increase that it will bring your company, exceptional customer service determines your future successes in business. Exceptional customer service speaks to the character of your employees, your business and ultimately you.

"Example isn't another way to teach, it is the only way to teach."
— Albert Einstein
German-born physicist who developed the special and general theories of relativity

"A leader leads by example, whether he intends to or not."
— Anonymous

CHAPTER 19

LEADERSHIP BY EXAMPLE

Leadership is the ability of a person to influence others and to obtain their willing cooperation and personal ownership, in order to achieve set goals and objectives required to reach a well-defined and articulated worthy vision; as well as guiding the way until the vision becomes a reality.

People in organizations pay more attention and follow what you do rather than what you say. There is no substitute, or a more powerful language, than leading by example. When people start imitating the professional and human qualities and traits that they see in you, the whole organization will start a path of transformation and your leadership qualities will be highly noted and appreciated.

In my definition of a leader, I stress various key qualities necessary for effective leadership:

1. A Leader Influences People

You can influence people through:
- Your character (#1 and most powerful tool)
- The authority of your position (title)
- Your unique skills and talents
- Your Charisma (special enthusiasm you have for people

with charm or a magnetic personality)
- Your age and experience
- Your historical performance
- How many people you have served or developed

2. A Leader Persuades to Obtain Willing Cooperation

Followers are attracted and motivated by the good examples of their leaders, examples they want to emulate and follow. People are visual in nature. They interpret and follow what they see. No wonder researchers say that more than 50% of our communication comes from our body language.

Your good example is one of the most powerful training tools you possess; in fact, your character is the most powerful teaching tool you have. When people see a character traits they want in themselves, they will follow you, in order to learn and become the desired trait which they see in you.

Jesus is the best example of leading by example. In his book, The Lost Art of Leadership (MileStones International Publishers), Dr. James B. Richards writes:

"The greatest leader who ever lived, Jesus of Nazareth, the Messiah, did not stand in Heaven and demand that people follow His orders. He became a man, lived among us and showed us how to live life at its fullest. His first invitation for training on His leadership team was simple: 'Follow Me!' He offered His follower the opportunity to see His teachings put into practice before deciding whether or not to accept a divine appointment. The model He lived was the proof of who He was and the process whereby He would develop His team."

For a true professional, there is nothing that will bring you more respect and recognition faster, than to model the healthy attributes and characteristics outlined in this book, leading the people around you to practicing them too.

3. A Leader Takes Personal Ownership and Responsibility

Our culture and present society is characterized by people

who don't want to take personal responsibility for their actions; they spend valuable time in pointing fingers, scapegoating and excuses.

A true professional takes responsibility for his mistakes, apologizes sincerely, takes responsibility for fixing the mistake, learns from the mistake, solves the mistake quickly and makes sure it doesn't happen again.

4. **A Leader Has Clear Goals and Sets Clear Objectives**
   - Write down on a piece of paper everything you want to be, to do or to have. Make sure the list is balanced in terms of physical, spiritual, social, career, family and financial goals. The list could be pretty long at this point.
   - Let your list sit for two days and come back to it. Review it, adding or deleting the items on the list.
   - At this point, take each item on your list and describe it with as much detail as you can, adding to it, including color, smells, size, how it feels, how it tastes, how it sounds. This technique is called "five sensing" and its originator was Walt Disney. The more rich in details and definition, the better the opportunity of your subconscious mind to "buy-in" to the vision.
   - Set realistic timetables for the completion of each of your goals.
   - Start working on the different tasks needed to accomplish the goal.
   - Review this list as often as you can every week, visualize it again and adjust it, as certain goals you originally set will lose appeal over time.

5. **A Leader Has a Well-Defined and Well-Articulated Vision**

Most people don't accomplish their goals because they approach them as "wish lists" rather than a project they have to work on. Some of us just don't believe we can accomplish big dreams, so why bother? The realization of dreams is hard work and requires a vision, a plan, strategies, timetables, daily work on the different tasks needed, periodic revision and course correction, perseverance and at the end, accomplishment. Just like a project; in fact, it is your life plan/project.

6. **A Leader Guides the Way**
   - Encourage the team during the "good" and the "bad."
   - Cast and recast the vision, constantly keeping it in front of everyone.
   - Coach the team on skills and character, serve as a sounding board, and provide the resources they need to perform at their best (training, people, financial, technology, etc.).
   - Train the people that report to you on how to mentor & develop other people.
   - Inspect what is expected.
   - Personally and sincerely care for the people on your team, and demonstrate it through your actions.

7. **A Leader Perseveres Until Achieving the Vision**

   Napoleon Hill said, "The majority of men meet with failure because of their lack of persistence in creating new plans to take the place of those which fail."

   The majority of men meet with failure because of their lack of persistence in creating new plans to take the place of those which fail.

"Our attitude toward life determines life's attitude towards us."
— John N. Mitchell

CHAPTER 20

KEEP AN ATTITUDE OF EXCELLENCE

A true professional has a constant commitment and attitude to doing things right the first time, as they recognize the high cost of a double effort, by having to go back to do a job for a second time in order to correct mistakes and quality issues.

Excellence is the attitude or mindset of quality, of excelling. It is superiority, or the desire to be the best you can be at a high level of performance. Excellence is considered to be a value by most organizations, but achieved by few.

The pursuit of excellence is not to be confused with a quest for pre-eminence, and is not about competition or about "outdoing others," which is based in a selfish motive.

Excellence is not success. Success means being the best. Excellence means being your best. Success is about the outcome of a goal, or eminence; it means being better than everyone else (like a competition).

Excellence means being better tomorrow than you were yesterday; it is competing with yourself to be the best every day that you can be.

Success means exceeding the achievements of other people. Excellence means matching what you do with the potential of what you can do or be, regardless how small or humble the task is. It is a mindset, an attitude. It is not something you do, but it is a habit.

Excellence calls for doing things right the first time. It is about practicing a skill until you master it; it's about learning new skills and upgrading the skills you already have. It is about trying again and again until you have it right and making your best effort every time.

Personal excellence is about change, about taking risks; it is about making mistakes and learning from them and correcting them; it is also about loving to learn new things, daily; it is about curiosity, adaptation and paying attention to details.

A key to excellence is to set goals (see chapter 18) and to ask for feedback and even criticism, which can help you to be better and better every day.

Leadership by example, listening to people and living your life with enthusiasm are all the attributes of professionals who possess the attitude of gratitude and excellence.

Having fun while you are pursuing excellence is an attitude you should practice. Encouraging others to be their best is a vital component of a team. Most of us need to be motivated and challenged to be our best and we admire the people who take the time to care about us.

As you do your best to create a habit and an attitude for excellence, you will stumble and sometimes you will fall. But man's character is measured, not by the amount of times he falls, but by the amount of times he bounces back when he falls.

"The secret of health for both mind and body is not to mourn for the past, worry about the future, or anticipate troubles, but to live in the present moment wisely and earnestly."

— Buddha
Hindu Prince Gautama Siddharta, the founder of Buddhism
563-483 BC

CHAPTER 21

HEALTH

This chapter is not intended to be a medical treatise on health, but rather a way to create consciousness on the importance of improving your health habits, in order to help your body function within the highest degree of productivity, thus, enabling you to live a fuller quality of life.

A true professional recognizes that in order to be productive they have to stay alive and in good health. Self-discipline and the development of good habits in eating and exercising keeps you alert, energetic, and significantly improves your attitude, (as well as prolongs your life span).

Staying healthy is not a sacrifice or an optional action; it is a choice and a lifestyle. An unhealthy or a dead manager makes a poor manager.

A healthy mindset starts with the attitude and awareness that without it, you won't be able to be happy or make anyone else around you happy.

Health is the state of balance between the absence of illness (normal body functions), the ability to cope with your environment and daily life (stress levels and psychological state) and how physically fit you are (optimum body wellness). All these factors determine a healthy quality of life.

Health is maintained and improved through physical fitness, weight loss, healthy eating, stress management training and avoiding smoking and abuse of harmful substances, among other things. The science and practice of medicine can definitely improve health, especially when your state of wellness is threatened or in danger.

Dr. John Tickell, a world-renowned medical researcher in the area of stress, says, "that stress is predictable and preventable. We all have the external pressures that life brings: mortgage payments that are due, personal conflicts, loss of love or a loved one, deadlines, etc. I call those external pressures opposing forces, as generally speaking, you don't necessarily want those events to happen, but they happen and you can't control them."

You can choose to respond or react to such external opposing forces or pressures. If you choose to react, it means that you have chosen to reply by using an emotion (anger, sadness, indignation, love, fear, etc.) in response to the pressure. If you choose to respond to the pressures of life, it means that you have chosen to be more rational, taking the time to look for explanations and to understand the source and reasons of the pressures, before you formulate any type of reply.

In both cases, you have little or no control over the pressures of life, but you do have control over the choice that you make on how to deal with the pressures. Either you choose to emotionally react or rationally respond; it's your choice. The choice that you make in this area determines the amount and the intensity of stress you live your life under and the strain you submit your body and immune system to.

Fear and worries are significant factors that destroy inner peace, and bring disharmony and stress. Emotional responses can be caused by anticipation or awareness of danger. Fears can be real (a truck is coming your way), or irrational (I have to a pain in my chest, what if I'm having a heart attack or have lung cancer). Real fears are a useful tool, as it helps you avoid danger; but irrational fears only serve to paralyze you to function properly in this world.

Worrying, which is negative goal setting, is thinking and dwelling on those things you don't want to happen and feeling fearful in advance, instead of thinking and dwelling on the things you do want to happen and thus, feeling the corresponding emotions.

Everybody has faith in something. If it is faith in yourself exclusively, then you will have a very limited view of what you can and cannot do. If your faith is in a God that created the universe, the complexities of the human body, and who still is in control of everything, your view of what you can or can't do as you submit to Him, as His instrument, could be unlimited (my personal view).

If you feel that you have to control everything you will live in a constant state of stress, worry and fear. But if you believe that the Creator of all there is actually is in control of everything and He is on call to hear your needs and help you, if you trust Him and let Him work, He will give you a peace and confidence like you have never experienced before. Studies show that people that believe in something greater than themselves (God) are healthier, happier and heal faster, than the people who believe that they are their god or that there is no God.

You act on your beliefs. We become what we think more prevalently. Therefore, you must feed yourself with the right thoughts and belief system, in order to fill your mind with the needed self-affirmations and positive thoughts to get you where you want to be in life.

For instance, what you eat determines how your body functions, in the same way that what you put in an engine (sand or gas) determines how well the engine runs. Healthy, balanced meals (balanced in proteins, carbohydrates, fiber) in moderate portions, will increase your energy, keep your body healthier and increase your lifespan. You will be more alert, think faster and more clearly, you can work longer hours without getting tired, and have a better attitude.

Exercise is also an essential health component. Make sure you spend at least 30 minutes, 3 times a week, in some kind of physical activity. More would be better, but this is the minimum recommended amount. Running, lifting weights, yoga, or walking on a treadmill are excellent ways to increase your metabolism and strengthen your heart.

Major health killers include fear and worry (stress), addictions and chemical dependencies, anger, poor eating habits, sleep deprivation, lack of exercise, overwork, lack of inner peace, etc.

You cannot live your life without the help of people and/or things around you bringing balance to your life. Simply put, taking time to maintain a healthy lifestyle through exercise, healthy eating habits, and faith in God provides an environment for you and those around you to thrive in. Reduce worry and stress in your life, and find the joy again that will bring you long-lasting life.

"Teamwork is the ability to work together toward a common vision. The ability to direct individual accomplishments toward organizational objectives. It is the fuel that allows common people to attain uncommon results."

— Unknown

Chapter 22

Teamwork

Ronald Reagan once said, "There's no limit to what a man can do or where he can go if he doesn't mind who gets the credit." There are no solo players or stars on a team; there is no "I" in the word "team." Helping other team members to score and succeed is the mark of great players and leaders and it is one of the fastest ways to catapult a department or a company forward. Unselfishness is the key to help other people grow, which will directly reflect and impact your own growth.

Love, the unselfish quality of wanting to help others, is the foundation to effective teambuilding. When you love you trust and when you trust you bond. Nothing pulls a team closer than love and trust. And there is nothing that builds loyalty more than love and trust.

As a team, you are like a machine; each part is necessary and has to work properly for the entire machine to work efficiently. Each team is like a living organism and each part is made up of the different gifts, talents and personalities God has given each member of the team to work efficiently. Some of us are artistic, some logical and some analytical, while others are social and outspoken, some are comfortable working fast and others are at their best working a little slower. All team member styles and velocities are necessary for the team to work at the peak of productivity.

When you are part of a team, you share the credit; you don't strive for personal credit. A team member fully understands his role and the role of the other members of the team, in relation to the "big picture" of the organization. There is no internal competition on a team, as internal competition doesn't produce positive results for anyone.

Together You Accomplish More

The word "synergy" comes from the Greek synergos, which means working together. Synergism is a condition in which the total combined effort of a team is greater than the sum of the single efforts of individuals. Team performance is an unselfish attitude where you work together for the accomplishment of the end result, the goal, and not for your own glorification or self-gratification.

Teamwork is a group of people who share a commitment of working together, relying on the interdependence of each team member to ensure the team's overall performance, in order to meet or exceed the set goals.

A team is an integral unit, working toward organizational objectives and goals for the good of the organization or team as a whole, rather than an aggregate of individuals working selfishly on independent goals.

The following are a few of my favorite quotes on teamwork:

"Individual commitment to a group effort — that is what makes a team work, a company work, a society work, a civilization work."

— Vince Lombardi
American Football coach

"The leaders who work most effectively, it seems to me, never say "I". And that's not because they have trained themselves not to say "I". They don't think "I". They think "we"; they think "team". They understand their job is to make the team function. They accept responsibility and don't sidestep it, but 'we' gets the credit ... . This is what creates trust, what enables you to get the task done."

— Peter F. Drucker

"In the end, all business operations can be reduced to three words: people, product and profits. Unless you've got a good team, you can't do much with the other two."

— Lee Iacocca

"No problem is insurmountable. With a little courage, teamwork and determination a person can overcome anything."

Unknown

'When a team outgrows individual performance and learns team confidence, excellence becomes a reality."

— Joe Paterno

American football coach

"Teamwork is so important that it is virtually impossible for you to reach the heights of your capabilities or make the money that you want without becoming very good at it."

— Brian Tracy

Author, Lecturer and American television host

"It's not the style that motivates me, as much as an attitude of openness that I have when I go into a project."

— Herbie Hancock

CHAPTER 23

EFFECTIVE PROJECT MANAGEMENT

A true professional knows how to turn ideas into reality. Nothing happens until you implement. The ability to implement (to become a doer, rather than just a dreamer) is one of the most important and powerful skills a professional can possess. You must know how to properly execute in order to turn your dreams and vision into reality.

Project Implementation

Implementation can take the form of ideas, learned concepts and skills, business processes, customer service programs and projects.

Project management is the process of planning, organizing, and managing tasks (an activity that has a beginning and an ending; projects are made up of sum total of tasks) and resources (money, time, people, equipment, forms, software, skills, etc.) to accomplish a defined objective, usually within time constraints (deadlines), resources, or cost.

In its basic form, a project plan can be simple; for example, a list of tasks and their start and finish dates written on a notepad. Or it can be more elaborate with hundreds of tasks and resources and a projected budget of millions of dollars.

The key to successful project implementation is the (1)

breaking of the project into easily, more manageable tasks, (2) scheduling the tasks, (3) communicating with the team or people responsible for the execution of the various tasks, and (4) tracking, supervising and controlling the tasks as work progresses.

1. The three major factors affecting a project are:
2. Time: The time needed to complete the project which is reflected in your project scheduling.
3. Money: The project budget, based on the cost of the resources: the people, equipment, and materials required to do the tasks.
4. Scope: The goals and tasks of the project and the work required to complete them.

Every time you adjust any of these elements, it will affect the other two.

The following outline describes the questions you must understand and answer for a successful project implementation process:

Why

- Why are we doing this? What is the main objective and benefit?

Who

- Who will do it?

What

- What resources do I need to implement and organize this idea?
  » Money
  » Time
  » People
  » Equipment
  » Forms, software
  » Skills
  » Communication tools (memo, e-mail, verbal, story

board)

When

- When would be a realistic date to complete this project?
- When should each task be completed in order to complete the project on time?

Where

- Events (activities) and places which need to take place; order activities in sequence (this has to happen, before these other things happen).

How

- In various phases or just one phase?
- Outline the detailed tasks (steps) needed to complete a phase (a number of tasks completes a phase; a number of phases completes a project).
- How much will the project cost?
- How are you going to track the progress of the project?
- How and how often will you report the progress of the project and to whom?
- How will you supervise and control the project (inspect what you expect) in respect to budget, people's performance, progress (timeline) and quality?

Rules for Effective Project Management

1. Clearly define the project.
   - Decide how it looks, smells, sounds, feels and tastes like (five-sensing technique introduced by Walt Disney)
2. Set a clear project goal.
   - What is the ultimate outcome?
3. Define the project objectives.
   - What is the purpose, reason, strategies and ideas to reach the goal?

1. Establish the activities (tasks) necessary to complete each objective.
2. Establish the time schedule estimates, working it backwards from the date the project must be completed.
3. Determine the resources you will need in each phase.
4. Plan your communications with people assigned to the project.
5. Empower the project team members to make decisions, as well as mistakes.
6. Encourage risk taking and creativity.
7. Track the progress and manage the schedule and budget/cost.
8. Keep everyone connected and informed on the progress and changes of the project.
9. Manage the resources to make sure everyone is doing their job, encourage them and find out if they need anything from you to complete their assigned responsibilities.
10. Manage the project scope and make adjustments as needed.
11. Manage the risks as they arise.
12. Report project status and progress to everyone involved.

And always remember, winners do what losers don't like to do. Nothing happens until we execute; so…just do it!

"You must take personal responsibility. You cannot change the circumstances, the seasons or the wind, but you can change yourself. That is something you have charge of."

— Jim Rohn
American speaker and author
Famous for motivational audio programs for business and life

"Man must cease attributing his problems to his environment, and learn again to exercise his will — his personal responsibility in the realm of faith and morals."

— Albert Schweitzer
German medical missionary, theologian, musician and philosopher
1952 Nobel Peace Prize
(1875-1965)

CHAPTER 24

TAKING PERSONAL RESPONSIBILITY

Personal responsibility is the acknowledgement that you are solely responsible for the choices in your life. There are no victims. You are responsible for what you choose to feel, think, or do. In fact, this is the only thing in life you can control: your thoughts and actions.

Emotional maturity and professionalism is shown when you accept to choose the direction of your life and choose not to blame others or make up excuses for the choices you have made. You must stop the defensive thoughts and rationalizations for why others are to blame for who you are, what you do, what has happened to you or what you are going to become. You are the architect of your circumstances; you are totally responsible for determining who you are, and choosing the choices that affect your life and circumstances.

One of the most important lessons you learn in life is that of developing the habit of taking responsibility and facing the consequences of your actions.

Your attitudes in life determine your feelings about any events or actions that come your way, no matter how negative they seem to be. When you choose positive attitudes to deal with life, you start realizing you don't have to depend on others to make you feel good about yourself.

As you enter adulthood and maturity, you determine how your self-esteem will develop, if you don't permit that other people, circumstances, or the culture, define who you are. By ceasing and refusing to feel sorry for the "bad deal"' you have been handed, you can start taking hold of your life and give it direction and significance.

When you let go of your need to take responsibility for the actions of others, you will start feeling a tremendous sense of relief and freedom from this self-imposed overburden. This will benefit your health and emotional well-being immediately. As for those whose responsibilities you have consistently carried upon yourself, it could become a great opportunity for them to learn to take responsibility for their own lives.

Many people that have adversely affected your life did so out of their limitations of their knowledge, background, and awareness. As you understand this truth and as you let go of blame and anger toward those in your past who did the best they could but fell short or were deliberate in their actions, you will be able to work out anger, hostility, pessimism, and depression over past hurts, pains, abuse, mistreatment, and misdirection.

Failure to accept personal responsibility for your own choices in life will result in negative consequences, such as becoming overly dependent on others for recognition, approval, affirmation, and acceptance, hostility, anger, and depression over how unfairly you have been or are being treated.

If left unchecked, you may become fearful about taking risks or making decisions as you grow to be overwhelmed by disabling fears, thus, failing at the enterprises you take on in life. You become unsuccessful in personal relationships as you are emotionally or physically unhealthy, which can lead to addictions to unhealthy substances, such as alcohol, drugs, food, or addictive behavior such as gambling, compulsive shopping, sex, smoking, over work, etc.

Clearly, people who don't accept personal responsibility are seen by others as immature, incompetent, and unworthy of respect.

In order to accept personal responsibility you need to develop the ability to take risks in life and accept the consequences of these risks, whether positive or negative.

Recognize that you choose your responses to the people, circumstances, actions, and events in your life. Make a conscious effort to let go of anger, fear, blame, mistrust, and insecurity and the only and best way to be successful is to review your spiritual beliefs and learn what your relationship with God is.

If you recognize that you are struggling with not taking personal responsibility, seek out and accept help for yourself. This is a sign of strength, not of weakness. Rebut illogical beliefs that will help overcome your fears by making constant positive affirmations about yourself. Recognize that you are the master of the choices you make.

It is essential that you take off the masks of pretensions and behavior characteristics behind which you hide your low self-esteem and realize that you are solely in charge and responsible for the direction your life takes.

"Rudeness is the weak man's imitation of strength."
— Eric Hoffer
American writer
1902-1983

"A little rudeness and disrespect can elevate a meaningless interaction to a battle of wills and add drama to an otherwise dull day."
— Bill Watterson
American author of the comic strip Calvin & Hobbes, b.1958

CHAPTER 25

AVOIDING RUDE BEHAVIOR

Rudeness is defined as lacking social refinement. The message behind rudeness is one of ignorance and indifference of good social manners and intentional discourtesy. It is a message of self-centeredness and selfishness. It reflects a lack of polish and gentleness.

Rudeness is shown by word, action and inaction. Rudeness of word is when you verbally are unpolished, cursing, using street language or offensive language; telling bad taste jokes; being too personal in conversations with people you don't have a personal, intimate relationship with; using vulgar language or words or attitude; talking at the same time others are talking; constantly interrupting conversations; or talking in a loud voice tone.

Inaction rudeness includes those actions and demeanors which disrespect and diminish people, such as: being abrupt and/or "in your face"; not being courteous; ignoring people's feelings and concerns; impoliteness; or lack of civility.

Rudeness of inactions includes those behaviors of omissions that send a message, without words, of rudeness to people. It's more about what you don't do, than what you do. Behaviors such as not returning phone calls (including sales calls); not paying attention to people when they are talking; ignoring people ("cold shoulder treatment"); being inconsiderate and uncaring; and lastly, apathy.

Rudeness turns people off at the speed of a bullet. The following is a list of rude behavior to avoid at all costs, if you want to win the respect of others:

- Not returning phone calls or messages.
- Answering your cell phone or checking messages in the middle of a conversation.
- Reading or replying to text messages or taking cell phone calls in the middle of a conversation, a business meeting, or a luncheon.
- Flossing in public.
- Loud talking on the cell phone while in public.
- Using bad language.
- Using slang terms like "B.S." and "Freaking".
- Yawning without covering your mouth.
- Yawning in the middle of a meeting.
- Talking with your mouth full of food.
- "Me first" aggressive actions.
- Burping in public.
- Typing on the computer while talking with someone on the phone.
- Interrupting while others are talking.
- Beginning e-mails without a "hello" or "good morning" greeting.
- Not sending a "Thank You" note when someone has done something for you.
- Not acknowledging receipt of a gift, package, letter, etc. sent to you.
- Misspelling words in your e-mail communications.
- All selfish behavior.
- Indifference in customer assistance (not making eye contact).
- Aggressive driving.
- Being frequently late to appointments and meetings.
- Chewing gum in a professional environment.
- Not looking directly and attentively at the speaker while in a conversation.
- Filing or clipping nails while in a meeting (even an informal one).

"Peace is not absence of conflict; it is the ability to handle conflict by peaceful means."

— Ronald Reagan
American 40th US president (1981- 89)
(1911-2004)

CHAPTER 26

CONFLICT RESOLUTION

Webster's dictionary defines conflict as: (a) competitive or opposing action of incompatibles: antagonistic state or action (as of divergent ideas, interests, or persons) (b): mental struggle resulting from incompatible or opposing needs, drives, wishes, or external or internal demands.

Conflict has to do with the way individuals handle grievances and clashes in opinions and right and wrong judgments. Conflict resolution is the process of resolving a dispute, a difference or a disagreement.

The process of conflict resolution doesn't need to be contentious or aggressive. On the contrary, the best resolutions are the ones that are handled in a civil, non-aggressive "brain storming" style.

One of the most effective techniques for conflict resolution is when you discover and unselfishly and freely share information about another's needs, perceptions and values through a creative thinking process, which adequately addresses each party's interests so that at the end, both parties are fully satisfied with the outcome.

For this process to work, each party must come to the table with honesty, transparency and without the attitude of taking advantage of the other party's provided information to achieve one-sided gains. The process should be totally focused on coming up with creative solutions that will solve each party's needs and must be completely unemotional.

The following is a summary of the process to conflict resolution:

1. Write a brief list with a description of the issues that you want to resolve, so you can gain understanding of what you want and why you want it and how it affects you if you don't have it. For example, if you want the other party to stop a certain behavior, you must start by clearly defining what is the behavior that you want the other person to stop doing; why or how you feel each time the person repeats the behavior; and how his/her behavior affects you personally.
2. Mutually share the information with the other party — in order to fully gain understanding of the content (issues and needs) and the intent (feelings) of each other.
3. Ask as many questions as possible — in order to gain understanding of each other's needs.
4. Start a creative thinking session — verbalizing and writing down every idea that comes to your mind, without rationalizing or making judgments of the idea. The more ideas you come up with from the "gut" the better. Usually the instinctive or "gut" thinking ends up being the best ideas.
5. Take control of your emotions — this is a process designed to come up with solutions and to harmonize each other's needs, not to think selfishly or to "score" points to get what you want. Keep in mind that this is not an adversarial process, but a creative thinking process. It is an unselfish, understanding-gaining and solution- oriented process and not an egocentric one.
6. Separate ego from the issues (it's not about you personally, but about problem solving).
7. Use a conversational style during the process — use humor, analogies, accepting and understanding language. Ask for clarification (respond), rather than jumping into emotional conclusions (reacting).
8. Choose the best ideas — create consensus about which idea

or combination of ideas best meets each other needs. Now is the time to rationalize, analyze and reduce the ideas to the ones that best meets each other's needs.
9. Build mutually beneficial agreements — after coming up with a final list of ideas, write them down with specific instructions on how to implement the ideas, as well as specific resources needed, along with time frames.
10. You may have to initiate another creative thinking exercise to come up with specific ways to implement the ideas.
11. Generate options or alternate plans — in case the original ideas to be implemented don't work according to expectations. This method forces your thinking in different directions. Make sure that you remain flexible, considering all options and setting realistic expectations.

"Knowledge is power when it comes to boundaries. Those who do not know the boundaries are destined to cross them. People have been eaten for doing so!"

— Unknown Author

CHAPTER 27

BOUNDARIES

Learning about boundaries in your personal and business relationships is of the utmost importance, as boundaries allow you to know when you will "cause offense" to someone, and when someone "offends" you and how to respond to it in a healthy manner. Boundaries allow you to have your own personal space and rules of engagement. When someone crosses your relationship boundary, you may go through the emotions of anger, as you may feel threatened or hurt.

Therefore, establishing healthy boundaries for yourself and your partners, allows your relationships to be constructive, functional and healthy.

Boundaries are about knowing how to have healthy relationships and interactions with others. In an employment situation, most employees know that stealing from the company is grounds for ending the employment relationship. Crossing the "honesty boundary" through theft can cause termination of employment. Crossing other relationship boundaries can bring about consequences that are just as harsh.

The following points will help you in beginning to set healthy personal boundaries:

1. Make a written decisive list of what you want and don't want from people. A good idea is to classify the boundaries by generalities, as well as boundaries for specific people, relationships or circumstances. The boundaries you need to work on will be revealed to you as you think of those things
2. that frustrate, anger, or hurt you. Memorize this list and make them part of your values.
3. Educate or inform people (in a matter-of-fact way) what they are doing, that crosses over your set boundaries. Just inform them. Come to a decision to be extremely perceptive about boundaries and to be constructive about communicating and enforcing them.
4. Decide the consequences of each violation. If the violation continues, tell them specifically what you want and don't want, why, and how you feel about it. If it still persists, warn them how you will separate yourself from them and/or their negative behavior, either temporarily (while it continues), or if necessary, permanently. If the violation still continues, distance yourself as you said you would, preferably short term and long term when necessary. Most importantly, you must be willing, ready and determined to enforce the consequence resulting from the violation.

At the beginning, particularly for the people who've been in your life and have lived under your old "boundary-less life", your new boundaries may be hard on them. They may over-react by counter-attacking, possibly with a "guilt trip", or other manipulation tactics. Remember, change is difficult for most people.

The key is to be as matter-of-fact, emotionless and straightforward as possible when you are defining and setting your limits with them.

Boundaries in Business

The following information will help you in starting to set boundaries in business and within a professional setting.

Sexual Harassment

Behavior that may, at first, start as a joke becomes sexual harassment when it is (1) unwelcome (by either men or women); (2) becomes persistent; or (3) creates a hostile, unfriendly, or intimidating environment. Such behavior could be verbal, nonverbal or physical.

Make a strong commitment to never cross the boundary of sexual harassment in any of its manifestations. Not only could you will be exposing yourself as a sexual harasser, but you will also be exposing your company to a lawsuit (not to say that you will, more than likely, be fired).

Friendships in the Workplace

Many people in the workplace confuse being friendly with being friends. Being friendly and amicable implies just a disposition to live on good terms with others and to be helpful.

On the other hand, friendships you develop at work are fundamentally different from personal friendships. A job provides financial security and if forced to choose between keeping your source of income and a friendship, most people would choose to keep their job. You have a lot more at stake when choosing to enter into a workplace friendship.

The right group of friends can be a great influence on your career. The wrong group can get you fired. A true professional recognizes the difference between being friendly and thinking that because people are civil and friendly, they are your "buddies", as they know that crossing this boundary may be fatal to their career.

Monster.com provides the following advice:

- Be discreet about your friend's confidences, and think carefully about the type of information you choose to divulge.
- If you think your friendship puts you or your friend in a compromising position on the job, talk about it. If necessary, withdraw yourself from situations that might be a conflict of interest.
- Find out if your company has a policy regarding workplace

friendships and follow the rules.

Abusive Behaviors

The first step toward an abusive situation is where one person relinquishes control over the other one.

- Those Who Control Through Criticism
    - » People that make other people feel like they never do anything right. Nothing is ever good enough.
    - » An attitude that their way is the only right way.
- Those Who Control Through Moodiness and Anger Threats
    - » People that expect other people to read their minds and lose their temper when others cannot do so.
    - » When people give others the "silent treatment", expecting others to have the ability to figure out what they have done wrong and to know how to fix it.
- Those Who Control Through Denying Your Perceptions
    - » When people act very cruelly and then say to you that you are too sensitive and cannot take a joke.
    - » People that often break promises and then claim to have never made the promise.
- Those Who Control by Ignoring Our Needs and Opinions
    - » People that act like others opinions are not important, are stupid, or not welcomed.
- Those Who Control Through Decision Making
    - » Bosses that want to make all the decisions and don't empower other people to make decisions or take risks.
- Those Who Control Through Money
    - » When bosses manipulate and control by threatening not to give you a raise if you don't comply or make sure to remind you that the reason why you are eating is because of the money they provide for you.
- Those Who Control Through Shifting Responsibility

- » Always blaming others for everything that happens, never taking personal responsibility for anything
- Those Who Gossip
  - » Some people feel powerful as information brokers; they want to let everyone know that they are "in the loop" on everything that's happening around the workplace and they thrive by doing this.

    —Rumors can be incredibly disruptive and destructive within an organization. A lack of information or the wrong information can get rumors started, contrary to forthright, honest explanations, which will usually stop them.

    —It is important that as a professional you recognize and clearly differentiate between information sharing and gossip; also that you immediately separate from it and chose not to participate when you hear it. First and foremost, don't repeat what you hear.

Violence or Threatening or Abusive Behavior

Workplace violence, verbal or physical, which includes threats or actual abuse only escalate with time and are never excusable. Never permit anyone to abuse you verbally. This is a boundary that no one should ever cross in the workplace. However, if they do, you should, in no uncertain terms, tell them that their behavior is not acceptable and what will be the consequence the next time that they cross the line.

If you think this couldn't happen in your company, think again — it's estimated by the Occupational Safety and Health Administration (OSHA) that annually, two million Americans are victims of workplace violence annually.

Dishonesty and Theft

Dishonesty and theft includes: the theft of time, office supplies, and the use of office equipment for personal projects (without permission), lying or calling in sick to take a day off, taking petty cash money for personal use, false (or padding) expense reports, and using the company's computer for sending personal e-mails and surfing the Web.

Security experts say as many as 30 percent of workers steal, resulting in an estimated loss of $50 billion a year from U.S. companies; thus contributing to as many as one-third of business bankruptcies.

Substance Abuse

Substance abuse is more widespread than most employers realize. The U.S. Department of Health and Human Services estimates that from 6% to 11% of adults are substance abusers. Substance abuse costs U.S. employers an estimated $100 billion a year. Illegal drugs have led financially desperate employees to commit fraud, as well as committing violent behavior in the workplace.

"Never hire or promote in your own image. It is foolish to replicate your strength and idiotic to replicate your weakness. It is essential to employ, trust, and reward those whose perspective, ability, and judgment are radically different from yours."

— Unknown Author

CHAPTER 28

GETTING HIRED

I find it amazing how many job candidates portray or "act as if" they are not really interested in being hired. With the advent and increasing popularity of on-line recruitment, this attitude, as well as, the lack of professionalism has been increasing exponentially.

Recently, our company had three openings for high-level sales position. Upon calling the candidates for an interview, I was baffled at the amount of candidates that asked us "what was the position they were called for?". I call these types of candidates "resume spammers, or fishers". They blindly send a barrage of resumes, without any thought or particular consideration, expecting that some employer will "bite" and call them.

On another occasion, one candidate asked me for the link to the recruitment ad we posted, which was on one of the most popular online job search sites;... incredible!

A candidate that doesn't even know, or keep track of the companies they have applied to, shows a perception of apathy, arrogance, lack of professionalism (and denotes a measure of immaturity), ignorance, as well as lack of preparation.

When looking for a job:
- **Get organized**-have a list of every company you have

applied to, the date you applied, the name of the position and kind of industry. Keep detailed records handy for when you receive a call, so you don't get caught off balance.
- **Read the ad twice and carefully**-know exactly what skills and attributes the ad is asking for. Don't send the resume to companies that you just read the headline and the first paragraph of the recruitment ad Show self-respect and respect for others by studying the ad and understanding the requirements of the position, before sending the resume.
- **Show interest and enthusiasm**-You will never have a second chance for a good first impression. When you answer a recruitment call, sound energetic, positive, eager, interested and grateful. Remember that your attitude will determine your altitude.
- **Always include an introduction/cover letter**-A resume shows your skills and experience; a cover letter shows your attitude. Take the time to write a well composed letter which reflects who you are and what it is that you will bring to the table of the organization. This may be your only opportunity to show your value.
- **If you can't make an interview appointment, call**-Never stand up an employer; this is a smaller world than you may think. Not canceling an appointment or showing up late is the psychological equivalent of the kid's expression "whatever", which denotes apathy, carelessness, disrespect and immaturity. You will never get a decent job reflecting that kind of attitude.
- **Don't rush to ask the about compensation package**-show that you respect your time and theirs. The salary or compensation package should be the first thing you're interested in, it's a mote point if you don't get past the first interview. Asking for money early on in the interview process, especially before you have the chance to show what it is that the potential new employer will be paying for, shows a selfish focus on money, rather than in showing them what you can contribute and how you can add value to their organization.

- **Don't interview the interviewer**-Don't ask questions early on the interview, unless they ask you if you have any questions. Don't confuse the roles; the employer is the interviewer; you are the interviewed candidate. You will be perceived as rude and manipulative, if you try to control the interview, especially in the first interview.
- **Make it short and to the point**- Listen attentively to the employer and their questions. Give short and concise answers to their questions. Don't go on in tangents and personal comments. Listen to the intent (what is what they mean), as well as the content (what is the subject or issue) of their questions. Understanding the intent and content of the speaker, and responding accordingly, is the foundation of effective communications.
- **Research, research, research**-Study carefully the company, as well as the industry of your prospective employer, so you can talk with intelligence and show that you know how to do your homework. By showing a basic knowledge of your future employer and their industry, you come across as a true professional, interested in taking the time to get to know them and have a foundational understanding of them.
- **Strengths and weaknesses**-understand what your strengths and weaknesses are (personal and professional) and don't be afraid to honestly and humbly verbalize them in a short sentence. Also be prepared to express, what you are doing to strengthen your weaknesses. This shows humility, strength of character and self-knowledge.
- **Follow every interview with a "thank you" note, personally handwritten**- stressing again that, if hired, you will be giving your 'all in all' and briefly stating just a few of your attitude attributes, which will make you the right candidate to be hired.
- **Come to all interviews looking "like the President"**-don't underestimate the importance of looking professional and conservative, business-like dress (unless you are applying for a position in an industry that casual dress is appropriate). It's always good to air on the side of professionalism. Please

refer to chapter for detailed guidelines.
- **Follow up**-to obtain an interview, be persistent, but not a pest. Call to find out: if they received your resume; to let them know that you are looking forward to an interview, as your qualifications perfectly match the requirements of the position; to ask if the position has already been filled; or to let them know that you are still available and interested in the position.
- **Don't criticize your previous employers**-this is a major mistake, as it shows disloyalty and presents you as a disgruntled employee and a gossip. If you don't have something positive to say about your former employers, say very little.
- **Be friendly, but not too familiar**-show respect, professionalism, a friendly demeanor, flexibility, eagerness, optimism. On one occasion, a candidate that I was interviewing for the first time over the phone called me "buddy"; that was the moment he automatically disqualified himself for the position

"The human being who lives only for himself finally reaps nothing but unhappiness. Selfishness corrodes. Unselfishness ennobles, satisfies. Don't put off the joy derivable from doing helpful, kindly things for others."

— B. C. Forbes
Scottish-born American editor and founder of Forbes Magazine
(1917) 1880-1954

Chapter 29

Let's Start With Our Identity

Have you ever asked yourself, why I am on planet Earth? Or, who am I? Why do I exist? Have you tried desperately to "fit in" in order to be accepted, respected and loved? We all struggle at one time or another with the issue of the need for significance in life: the search for meaning and purpose.

All too often we permit society, Hollywood, the culture and other people to define our happiness, or define who we are through their own belief that having a certain car, drinking certain beer, living in a certain neighborhood, having a certain title, wearing a certain fashion or designer's clothing, or buying a certain product will define who we are and/or make us "happy".

In our consumer driven society of instant gratification and false significance, we often struggle to buy things that we don't need to impress people we don't know with money we haven't earned, thus getting us into debt that we can't pay.

In a world where we are constantly competing with others by keeping score based on what we have, our social status, titles, etc., we have lost our perspective of what's really important in life. Many of us have a great confusion between quality of living (defined by the things we have) and quality of life (which is defined by our values, which determine who we really are; which is our character).

Many of us have tried many ways to fulfill this craving for significance: drugs and alcohol, sex, titles, success and achievement, overwork, sports, luxury cars, material things, wealth, popularity and fame, self-gratification in different ways, etc. In fact, the great paradox is that many things that start at to be fun or pleasurable result in a life of pain, divorce, financial disaster, disease, addictions and relationship problems. The dilemma lies in that significance is not possible unless what we do contributes to the well-being and the good of others.

True significance is not about what you do to make you feel better about yourself, or to impress others; it is about what you do to help others, or what you do for the benefit of a greater good. This truth is expressed by all major religions, but it is sadly the most overlooked principle in life. The core of significance in life is rooted in your motives and your attitudes toward others; not in what you do, but in what you believe and your unselfish actions.

It is very important to analyze who you are and what it is important in life before you set goals. You need to learn what it is that you identify with, before you are able to look for direction through goals in life. In order to reach goals with peace of mind and joy in life, you need to find goals that are consistent with whom you are and that take into consideration the common good.

You cannot force yourself to perform in a way that is not aligned with who you are. Failure in this area will bring disharmony, confusion, depression, anger, lack of motivation, chronic frustration and feelings of failure.

Many times we get so tangled and distracted in running the rat race that we don't seem to find time to examine our lives to gain understanding, through analyzing and defining the things that are really important in life to us; not for anyone else, but to us.

In Rick Warren's book, The Purpose Driven Life, which has sold over 23 million copies and listed as #1 best seller on the New York Times Best Sellers list for weeks, outlines five different values to bring purpose to your life, based on spiritual values, not cultural values.

Paraphrasing Warren's insight and the Bible as the source of those insights, he points out that:

1. You were created for God's pleasure, so the first purpose is to get to know who God is and to have a personal relationship of love with Him. To know God is to love Him and when you know God, you will start defining yourself based on who God says you are, rather than on what society, your parents, or the culture says you are or should be.
2. You were created as part of God's family, so your second purpose is to enjoy true and more significant friendships with the people God has placed in our lives.
3. You were created to become or model the Jesus of the Bible, which is to grow spiritually, to become (which is a lifelong process) unselfish, rather than to practice selfishness. To learn how to look for other people's good, rather than looking for self-gratification and thinking only in terms of "what's in it for me".
4. You were created for serving God, so your fourth purpose is to love "your neighbor" with actions of love. True love is not a feeling, but a deliberate action you choose to take which benefits other people even when you don't feel like it. It is a choice, not a feeling.
5. You were created for a mission; ultimately, your mission in life. Once you become friends with God and you start enjoying the benefits of true significance, which is to encourage other people in their search for significance, through sharing with them where you were and where you now are as a result of your newly found friendship with God. Sharing the gift that God gave you with others becomes your mission in life, which directs your actions of love, as you wish to share the gift of true significance with others.

Don't confuse your purpose in life with being religious or the lack of desire for material goals and possessions; it has nothing to do with that. A goal is what you do, while a purpose is why you do what you do; your motives. You can choose material possessions for self-gratification or you can choose to have the same material possessions for the benefit of others. The motives of why you want the possessions determine your true purpose.

You can choose to perform your job with the attitude that "I deserve better" or the belief that others are taking advantage of you. You hear yourself saying, "I'm not getting paid what I deserve" or "I work for a bunch of jerks."

This attitude, however, will not bring you success in life or the workplace. Instead, choose to be the best that you can be, realizing that God didn't make you a mediocre. You must be conscious and fully aware that you are an important member of a team. You must also be conscious that what you do in excellence helps other people in your department and ultimately in your organization.

The secret of job contentment is not in the circumstances, but in your attitude, in spite of the circumstances. Your attitude will determine your altitude in life and in the workplace. You are the only one who can choose to be a victim or to be a conqueror.

Most people have confused ideas of what their priorities in life should be. In many cases we live by the priorities others have set for us, instead of the priorities we have set for ourselves. The following list of priorities is in alignment with what most religions and great unselfish thinkers have taught us priorities in life should be:

Priority #1: Getting to know and love God (through the study of God, sharing, praying, meditation and living an attitude of gratitude toward God).

Priority #2: Family life, friends and family values (experience the love of God through your family and friends).

Priority #3: Helping and serving others (be good to others, just because God has been good to you).

Priority #4: Work (with a positive attitude of gratitude).

Priority #5: Rest (recharge your "batteries").

When any of these priorities are out of balance or out of order, sooner or later you will experience moral, financial, family, or relational bankruptcy. A balanced set of priorities through a committed relationship with your Creator will bring to your life love, joy, peace, patience, kindness, goodness, faithfulness, gentleness and self-control.

"If you have integrity, nothing else matters. If you don't have integrity, nothing else matters."
— Alan K. Simpson

"You are in integrity when the life you are living on the outside matches who you are on the inside."
— Alan Cohen

CHAPTER 30

INTEGRITY: ACTING WHAT YOU BELIEVE

You can't behave in a way that is contrary to what you believe; therefore, what you believe controls your behavior. Your life philosophy drives and controls your vision, passions and actions.

In this chapter we are going to discuss two major philosophical issues in the life of a professional: business ethics and the impact of your spiritual life (whether you believe in a Higher Power or not) and in your professional life.

I have always admired the ethics of some of the old tycoons which have shaped our modern society. Inspired in the work of James D. Newton and based on his book Uncommon Friends (highly recommended reading), published by Harcourt Brace & Co., I would like to focus and review the faith and life philosophy of five geniuses who were close friends: Henry Ford, Thomas Alva Edison, Harvey Firestone, Charles Lindberg and Dr. Alcxis Carrel (1912 Nobel Prize winner for his work on suturing of blood vessels and organ transplant).

When these five friends got together, they loved to talk about the common good, industry, spirituality and the purpose of life and many other principled and philosophical subjects that nourished their curiosity and intellect.

Henry Ford thought that the purpose of making money was

to help society as a whole and to provide service excellently and unselfishly. He said, "The purpose of money is to provide more opportunity to perform more service. Short-sighted businessmen think first of money, but service is what really makes or breaks businesses; without it, customers soon go somewhere else. Mr. Edison's first concern wasn't in making money." He continued, "What really interested him was inventing things the world needed."

"If money is your only hope for independence, you will never have it. It's our first duty to do the right thing, and this will earn us the right money". Isn't that a great principled statement?

An outstanding testimony on Henry Ford's character was written in a letter by Charles A. Lindbergh to Mr. Ford on June 1942. Mr. Lindbergh wrote, "You combine the characteristics that I admire most in men: success with humility, firmness with tolerance and science with religion. Possibly the thing I admire the most about you is that you have built one of the world's greatest industries without letting it change your own outlook and character." This is one of the greatest character tributes and evidence of respect a man can ever expect to receive.

Thomas Alva Edison is well known in history, not only by his genius, perseverance, and character, but for his long, relentless hours of hard work. One of his quotes which show this attribute reads, "All things come to him who hustles while he waits." He is also the best example of working for the needs of people, not for his own selfish purposes. He made the following statement to James D. Newton: "The secret of staying afloat is to create something that people will pay for. I didn't work at inventions unless I saw a market demand for them. I wasn't interested in making money as much as in being the first to invent something society needed. But if you do that, the money comes in."

Some quotes which define the depth of character and leadership skills of Harvey Firestone:

"Never be bullied into silence. Never allow yourself to be made a victim. Accept no one's definition of your life, but define yourself."

"The growth and development of people is the highest calling of leadership."

"Capital isn't that important in business. Experience isn't that important. You can get both of these things. What is important is ideas."

"You get the best out of others when you give the best of yourself."

"The secret of my success is a two word answer: Know people."

Charles Lindbergh, in similar principled statement, said, "We should see people as more important than things, the producer as more important than the product, peace of heart as more important than the prize of possession. That's what I believe as the balance of spirit, mind and body." He said, "When I'm flying I'm a materialist — until I get my feet on the ground. When a flyer runs into something beyond the control of his own mind and body he realizes very quickly that he's in the hands of an unseen power."

These great men were committed to moral principles and the greater good of society as a whole, because they understood the force and the source behind any good in humanity. Their faith in God was public and a witness of everything that was right and good in them.

Charles Lindbergh, in a memorable statement on commitment, said, "It comes down to this: I have found that when you make a deep commitment (to God), unforeseen forces come to your aid. Getting to the point of deciding is the hard part. Once you are there, it is simple, we experience a spiritual rebirth." He stated that, once we make a deep commitment, "something" gives us the power to resist what is contrary to our commitment.

He quoted the difference of "internal surrender, which is humility" as opposed to "external self-sacrifice, which is pride." He meant that internal submission to a Higher Authority to guide us and to take care of our lives and decisions brings humility, a desirable character attribute. On the other hand, those things that we do to feel better about ourselves, (external self-sacrifice) or those things that we do for other people to notice us, fosters pride and selfishness, which is an undesirable character trait.

Dr. Alexis Carrel said that he learned that "there is a power in the universe beyond man's intellectual grasp." He told Mr. Ford, "Henry, it is not a question of trying to persuade your intellect that God exists. Instead, try sitting quietly and just suppose God is there. Listen and see what thoughts come into your mind. In other words, let your intuition reveal truth to you. The thoughts that come might not be so much about God, but about us."

Mr. Lindbergh's wife, Anne, added that the most important commitment in life is the commitment to crucify our pride; "…a commitment to relinquish as much of your will as you understand your Creator; to the degree you know Him or recognize Him or trust Him, or whatever." She said that if we don't believe in God, then you can make an experiment. Ask God, "If you are real, make it clear what it is I should do in life." She said, "He will do exactly that; He will show you the steps you should take."

If you decide to conduct this experiment, don't expect bells and whistles to ring. But if tonight you make that decision with a sincere heart, a positive expectation, and genuine contrition for your past deeds, tomorrow morning you will know. The decision to put your life in the hands of God, to trust him and follow Him will have an extraordinary effect in your life and the same impact it has had in the lives of these great men and that they were so unashamedly public about.

The first time that Lindbergh got to his knees in prayer and said to God: "I have my ideals, but I can't live up to them. I don't have what it takes. Okay, I've loused things up — if you are there and can call the shots, here is my will and my life. You run it, you fly it." He said ,that from that moment on, he gained a spiritual insight and a sense of direction in life, like he had never known before.

Dr. Alexis Carrel, in conversation with his friends, shared with them the following statement: "Man does not live by bread alone (Luke 4:4); nor does society. Men need to keep equilibrium between material and spiritual nourishment." He added, "The point is to concentrate your attention on something beyond the self; then comes inner peace. The inner control only emerges from the acceptance of values such as love, honesty, purity of motive and regard for others."

He believed that man has become isolated as self-sufficient, independent beings, that they have made a mess out of the resources of the planet and ultimately of their own lives. He thought that men have lost their identities and purposes in life, thinking that the world and life revolved around them and that they have forgotten that they are surrounded by scores of people who affect each other's lives, for better or worse, with their actions.

What amazed and intrigued me the most is that these illustrious pioneers of science and industry freely and publicly talked about their faith as the fundamental nature of who they were.

Mr. Lindbergh, after the Second World War, was touring a concentration camp; he was puzzled over the dichotomy of how people who have accomplished brilliant scientific achievements can live alongside with people of such human degradation and depravity. He thought: "Why have we allowed our pursuit of science to pervert the human spirit?" Indeed, our post-modern society has allowed and promoted science as something incompatible, therefore, separated from God, instead of science to teach us how things created by God work.

In today's materialistic culture it has become not fashionable or politically correct to talk about faith or about God. But it is our faith in God that brings meaning and direction to an otherwise senseless world. On our own, we don't have the power to follow any kind of moral code, but in God we have all the power we need.

Most of our founding fathers were God revering people. Brilliant minds and courageous men such as: Alexander Hamilton (signer of the Constitution); Daniel Boone (Revolutionary Officer and Legislator); Daniel Webster (Webster's Dictionary and Statesman); George Washington (our first President); James Madison (former President); John Adams (former President); John Marshall (Chief-Justice of the U.S. Supreme Court; Secretary Of State); Patrick Henry; Samuel Adams (Signer Of The Declaration); just to name a few; great men who believed in the Almighty and lived by faith and submission to God and were unapologetic for it.

How, then, can our relationship with God now be considered

as "intolerant", "closed minded" or "out of style"? Are we becoming "smarter" than our Founding Fathers and our greatest industrialists and brilliant minds; or perhaps just more proud and self-centered?

"Your legacy is the life you live and then leave behind. It includes everything you've ever done … and not done."

—Brian Mast
Author, business owner, and father

Chapter 31

Life Values and Legacy

Your core beliefs in life shape your value system. Your belief system consists of rooted assumptions (those things you have been trained to believe from childhood); cultural values (those things that you like and embrace from your cultural system); doctrinal values (those lessons about life, religion, politics and ideology, which establishes your judgment of right and wrong, best or worst); and aesthetics values (your conclusions about what is beautiful, ugly, pleasant or unpleasant to your eyes).

You can value materialism and selfishness, or spiritualism, love and unselfishness. Your quality of life and legacy will be the sum total of your choices in life.

The original purpose of this book, which is to preserve the original definition of professionalism as a character trait, is also a purpose that impacts and determines your legacy.

Allow me to review some of the previous chapter titles of this book:

- Be Reliable
- Learning is never over for the Professional
- Attitude
- Discipline

- Self-Control
- Temperance
- Unselfishness
- Ability to Train and Delegate
- Leadership by Example
- Attitude of Excellence
- Teamwork
- Taking personal responsibility
- Start with identity
- Integrity

These are an effective list of tips, secrets, patterns, and habits that will do anyone well who masters them. The combination of all of these character traits reflects upon you as a business, a professional, and an individual.

Each of this traits, when taken seriously and put into action, produce positive attitudes, success in business, and a legacy of a life driven by purpose. Sow seeds of success and expect success to grow as a result.

You, your belief system, your attitude, and your actions will determine if those seeds will continue to grow for generations after you and what will be the fruit of this continued growth.

Leaving a legacy is hard for anyone to forget and it undoubtedly leaves an unforgettable mark on your life. The legacy we leave to our children will speak of the life we have lived on this earth. It will speak volumes of the life we choose to lead now.

Therefore, leave a legacy that will speak honorably of your life and character and of the generations that will follow. Create a legacy of purpose!

OTHER BOOKS BY CANDIDO SEGARRA...

ARE YOU THE ARCHITECT OF YOUR CIRCUMSTANCES?

HOW THE QUALITY OF YOUR THOUGHTS AND CHOICES SHAPE YOUR CIRCUMSTANCES

★★★★★ Rated Five Stars By Forbes.com

CANDIDO SEGARRA

TESTIMONIALS

Forbes Book Reviews:

★★★★★

Excellent book with great information that is written in a concise manner that requires the reader to think. It could change your life in the most positive way.

amazon.com Book Reviews:

★★★★★ **Renew your mind!**,

This book takes no time to get down to the nitty-gritty and changes your perspective on circumstance. Our thought life really is more significant than we make it out to be and we ought to be more aware of its out-pouring into our daily lives.

Candido's sincerity in this book proposes a certain clarity that is difficult to find in other philosophical and theological publications. Although it is a short read it offers a lot to chew on. I recommend reading it a number of times.

It is often said that Dynamite comes in small packages. This is an example that makes the "cliché". An articulate weaving of spiritual and practical knowledge. In fact, you learn, if you didn't know already, that the spiritual truth of God is the most practical of all. If you already knew, you are reinforced and motivated to action in any endeavor in which you are involved. Segurra's writing will increase clarity, confidence and purpose in your life; all in a very quick read that you will enjoy and want to read over and over.

★★★★★ **Must Read!**

This book is very instructive on how we all are accountable for our destiny and how we can improve our relationship with our God by *applying the Bible's principles and taking ownership for our acts and thoughts.*

★★★★★ **Outstanding reading!!**
This book really was thought-provoking! It brought to the surface many issues I hadn't thought deeply about. I had to read it twice! I am already seeing life in a different way! It's worth your time...read it!

★★★★★ **Essential to your thought life!!!**
This book provides an in depth look at your quality of thought and how it affects the outcome of your life. It is a quick read that contains the keys to unlocking your potential. This is one of those that can change your entire life. Highly Recommended!!!

★★★★★ **Must read!**
An essential book for Christians. An insightful book on spirituality and circumstance.

★★★★★ **Great read!**
I thought this was a fantastic book. The author made strong points and backed it with clear concise thoughts. The reading was easy and thought-provoking. Highly recommend to all those interested in philosophy and religion. Easy to read and very thought-provoking! Candido masterfully weaves philosophy and religion together in captivating manner. Highly recommend!

★★★★★ **A real gem!**
It is often said that Dynamite comes in small packages. This is an example that makes the "cliché". An articulate weaving of spiritual and practical knowledge. In fact, you learn, if you didn't know already, that the spiritual truth of God is the most practical of all. If you already knew, you are reinforced and motivated to action in any endeavor in which you are involved. Segarra's writing will increase clarity, confidence and purpose in your life all in a very quick read that you will enjoy and want to read over and over.

★★★★★ **Unique, enlightening book!!**
This book bought to light issues of deep, penetrating thought. It truly makes you think! Possibilities of personal growth are endless! Worth the read!

★★★★★ **A must read**
Written in such a way that it gives you a spiritual awakening of your thought pattern. I highly recommend this book.

★★★★★ **Very Engaging**
This book helps you see beyond your immediate problems and see the 'bigger picture.' This book will help you to see the timeless principles in the Bible and then apply them to your life.

★★★★★ **Fantastic**
A book with a great blend of spiritual truths and practical thought.

Foresight Book Publishing™

A Revolution in Private Book Publishing
Turning Sermon Series Into Books

WWW.FORESIGHTPUBLISHINGNOW.COM

Foresight Management Development Program©

A world class management development training program to develop, equip and empower the best managers in America

WWW.FORESIGHTMDP.COM

www.ingramcontent.com/pod-product-compliance
Lightning Source LLC
Chambersburg PA
CBHW031248290426
44109CB00012B/483